Nature-Inspired Computing Paradigms in Systems

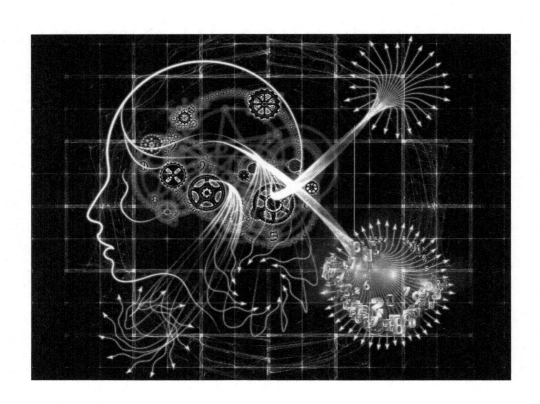

Nature-Inspired Computing Paradigms in Systems
Reliability, Availability, Maintainability, Safety and Cost (RAMS+C) and Prognostics and Health Management (PHM)

Edited by

Mohamed Arezki Mellal, Associate Professor,
Department of Mechanical Engineering, Faculty of Technology, M'Hamed Bougara University, Boumerdes, Algeria
CALCE (Center for Advanced Life Cycle Engineering), University of Maryland, College Park, MD, United States

Michael G. Pecht, Professor,
CALCE (Center For Advanced Life Cycle Engineering), University of Maryland, College Park, MD, United States

Series Editor: Fatos Xhafa
Universitat Politècnica de Catalunya, Spain

ACADEMIC PRESS
An imprint of Elsevier

ELSEVIER

Academic Press is an imprint of Elsevier
125 London Wall, London EC2Y 5AS, United Kingdom
525 B Street, Suite 1650, San Diego, CA 92101, United States
50 Hampshire Street, 5th Floor, Cambridge, MA 02139, United States
The Boulevard, Langford Lane, Kidlington, Oxford OX5 1GB, United Kingdom

Notices
Knowledge and best practice in this field are constantly changing. As new research and experience broaden our
understanding, changes in research methods, professional practices, or medical treatment may become
necessary.

Practitioners and researchers must always rely on their own experience and knowledge in evaluating and using
any information, methods, compounds, or experiments described herein. In using such information or methods
they should be mindful of their own safety and the safety of others, including parties for whom they have a
professional responsibility.

To the fullest extent of the law, neither the Publisher nor the authors, contributors, or editors, assume any liability
for any injury and/or damage to persons or property as a matter of products liability, negligence or otherwise, or
from any use or operation of any methods, products, instructions, or ideas contained in the material herein.

Library of Congress Cataloging-in-Publication Data
A catalog record for this book is available from the Library of Congress

British Library Cataloguing-in-Publication Data
A catalogue record for this book is available from the British Library

ISBN 978-0-12-823749-6

For information on all Academic Press publications
visit our website at https://www.elsevier.com/books-and-journals

Publisher: Mara Conner
Acquisitions Editor: Sonnini R. Yura
Editorial Project Manager: Emily Thomson
Production Project Manager: Swapna Srinivasan
Cover Designer: Vicky Pearson Esser

Typeset by SPi Global, India

Contents

CHAPTER 4   Evolutionary optimization for resilience-based planning for power distribution networks 47
Nariman L. Dehghani, Chi Zhang, and Abdollah Shafieezadeh

CHAPTER 5   Application of nature-inspired computing paradigms in optimal design of structural engineering problems—a review 63
Amit Kumar

Contributors

Roumaissa Boutiche
LMSS, Faculty of Technology, M'Hamed Bougara University, Boumerdes, Algeria

Nariman L. Dehghani
Risk Assessment and Management of Structural and Infrastructure Systems (RAMSIS lab), The Ohio State University, Columbus, OH, United States

Mohammad Ali Farsi
Reliability and standard group, A&S Research Institute, Ministry of Science, Research and Technology, Tehran, Iran

Abir Frik
LMSS, Faculty of Technology, M'Hamed Bougara University, Boumerdes, Algeria

Ikram Hamadache
LMSS, Faculty of Technology, M'Hamed Bougara University, Boumerdes, Algeria

Kai He
School of Engineering Science, University of Science and Technology of China, Hefei, China

Kasun Hewage
School of Engineering, University of British Columbia, Okanagan Campus, Kelowna, BC, Canada

Lisa Jackson
Department of Aeronautical and Automotive Engineering, Loughborough University, Loughborough, United Kingdom

Amit Kumar
Department of Information Technology, Rajkiya Engineering College, Ambedkar Nagar, Akbarpur, Uttar Pradesh, India

Lei Mao
School of Engineering Science, University of Science and Technology of China, Hefei, China

Mohamed Arezki Mellal
LMSS, Faculty of Technology, M'Hamed Bougara University, Boumerdes, Algeria; Center for Advanced Life Cycle Engineering (CALCE), University of Maryland, College Park, MD, United States

Rachid Ouache
School of Engineering, University of British Columbia, Okanagan Campus, Kelowna, BC, Canada

Rehan Sadiq
School of Engineering, University of British Columbia, Okanagan Campus, Kelowna, BC, Canada

Laxminarayan Sahoo
Department of Computer and Information Science, Raiganj University, Raiganj, India

Abdollah Shafieezadeh
Risk Assessment and Management of Structural and Infrastructure Systems (RAMSIS lab), The Ohio State University, Columbus, OH, United States

Amin Mohammadpour Shotorbani
School of Engineering, University of British Columbia, Okanagan Campus, Kelowna, BC, Canada

Qiang Wu
School of Engineering Science, University of Science and Technology of China, Hefei, China

Chi Zhang
Risk Assessment and Management of Structural and Infrastructure Systems (RAMSIS lab), The Ohio State University, Columbus, OH, United States

Editor biographies

Mohamed Arezki Mellal is an associate professor at the Department of Mechanical Engineering, Faculty of Technology, M'Hamed Bougara University, Algeria, and a visiting scholar at the Center for Advanced Life Cycle Engineering, Department of Mechanical Engineering, University of Maryland, College Park, MD, United States. Likewise, he was a visiting scholar at various universities. He has published in several journals and conference proceedings. He has edited five books and authored seven book chapters. He is a member of the Algerian National Laboratory for Maintenance Education in conjunction with the European Union (Erasmus+). He has also been a committee member for more than 70 international conferences. He serves as a regular reviewer for 18 SCI-indexed journals and an editorial board member in 7 peer-reviewed international journals. His research interests include developing new bioinspired optimization methods for solving engineering problems of system dependability, manufacturing, and energy efficiency.

Michael G. Pecht (30,000+ citations, 80+ H-Index) has a BS in physics, an MS in electrical engineering, and an MS and PhD in engineering mechanics from the University of Wisconsin. He is a professional engineer, an IEEE fellow, a PHM Society life fellow, an ASME fellow, an ASM fellow, an SAE fellow, and an IMAPS fellow. He served as editor in chief of IEEE Access for 6 years, as editor in chief of IEEE Transactions on Reliability for 9 years, editor in chief of Microelectronics Reliability for 16 years, and editor of Circuit World. He has also served on three US National Academy of Science studies, two US Congressional investigations in automotive safety, and as an expert to the US FDA. He is the Director of Center for Advanced Life Cycle Engineering (CALCE) at the University of Maryland (UMd), which is funded by more than 150 world's leading electronics companies at more than US$6 M/year. He is also a professor in applied mathematics at UMD. In 2008, he was awarded the highest reliability honor, the IEEE Reliability Society's Lifetime Achievement Award. In 2010, he received the IEEE Exceptional Technical Achievement Award for his innovations in the area of prognostics and systems health management.

Preface

Nowadays, competitiveness in all industrial sectors is due to the number of companies and the requirements of regulations and users. Industrial companies focus on development and acquisition of systems with a high level of dependability. However, it involves many challenges. During the last decades, various solution techniques have been proposed to deal with these challenges. Nature-inspired computing techniques have proved their effectiveness in solving hard engineering problems. The present work is part of nature-inspired paradigms in systems—RAMS+C (Reliability, Availability, Maintainability, Safety, and Cost) & PHM (Prognostics and Health Management).

The book is divided into eight chapters. Chapter 1 deals with the reliability optimization of a safety system in the power plant using gray wolf optimizer and the shuffled flog-leaping algorithm. Chapter 2 addresses the design optimization of the car side safety system using particle swarm optimization and gray wolf optimizer. Chapter 3 presents the basic principles of genetic algorithm and its application in RAMS. Chapter 4 uses evolutionary optimization for resilience-based planning in power distribution networks. Chapter 5 presents a review of the application of nature-inspired computing in optimal design. Chapter 6 uses artificial neural networks and genetic algorithms for fire safety strategies assessment. Chapter 7 applies artificial neural networks to proton exchange. Finally, Chapter 8 addresses reliability redundancy allocation problems with uncertainties using genetic algorithms and dual-connection numbers.

This book can be used by researchers, students, engineers, industrial companies, or any person interested in nature-inspired computation and RAMS+C & PHM.

Mohamed Arezki Mellal
Michael G. Pecht

Acknowledgment

The editors would like to thank the following reviewers:

Fausto Pedro García Márquez
Universidad Castilla-La Mancha, Spain

Harish Garg
Thapar Institute of Engineering and Technology, India

Payman Dehghanian
George Washington University, United States

Sameer Al-Dahidi
German Jordanian University, Jordan

Wei Wang
City University of Hong Kong, Hong Kong

Reliability optimization of power plant safety system using grey wolf optimizer and shuffled frog-leaping algorithm

Mohamed Arezki Mellal[a,b]**, Abir Frik**[a]**, and Roumaissa Boutiche**[a]

LMSS, Faculty of Technology, M'Hamed Bougara University, Boumerdes, Algeria[a] *Center for Advanced Life Cycle Engineering (CALCE), University of Maryland, College Park, MD, United States*[b]

1. Introduction

The world is witnessing great industrial developments in which the need for high-level operating facilities leads to great competition. In this context, the designers must devote their efforts to increase the reliability of the systems to increase the overall reliability of the facilities. The most common design objectives are (1) the maximization of the system reliability under the allowable system cost and other design limits, such as the weight and volume; (2) the minimization of the system cost under the allowable system reliability and the other design limits for the single-objective reliability optimization problems (ROPs); or (3) a combination of considerations, such as system reliability and cost for the multiobjective ROPs. System reliability could be improved using three main methods:

1. Redundancy allocation: add redundant components in parallel. This method could be employed using active or standby components. If the standby redundant components cannot fail until they are switched on, then it is called cold-standby strategy [1, 2]. If the standby redundant components can fail when they are switched off and have lower failure rates than the active components, it is called warm-standby strategy. In some references, the active component redundancy strategy is called hot-standby strategy [3, 4].
2. Reliability allocation: allocate reliability to the components and/or subsystems of the system to meet the overall required system reliability.
3. Reliability-redundancy allocation: a combination of the allocations 1 and 2.

This chapter focuses on the single-objective ROPs. The reliability-redundancy optimization problem of a power plant safety system is addressed using the grey wolf optimizer (GWO) and the shuffled frog-leaping algorithm (SFLA). It is organized as follows: Section 2 gives a literature review of some previous works related to the ROPs. Section 3 presents the ROP of the investigated power plant safety

Nature-Inspired Computing Paradigms in Systems. https://doi.org/10.1016/B978-0-12-823749-6.00008-8

system. The implemented GWO and SFLA are presented in Sections 4 and 5, respectively. Section 6 discusses the results obtained. Finally, the last section concludes the chapter.

2. Literature review

Several research works have been devoted to the ROPs. Refs. [5–7] are among the first papers published on this topic and the authors used the so-called classical mathematical method to solve the ROPs. During the last decades, most of the solution approaches were based on iterative computational intelligence methods that offer many advantages, such as the ability to handle hard problems, flexibility, good results, and reasonable computational time [8–12]. Several ROPs were reviewed in Refs. [13, 14]. This section presents a nonexecutive review of the literature due to the number of published works related to this topic.

Bicking [15] proposed a solution method based on genetic algorithms with evolutionary strategies (GMs). This method combines the principle of tracking the most suitable individuals and the genetic combinations for an elitist research mechanism. To prove the performance of the proposed method, four systems with various configurations were investigated and the results were compared to those of the simulated annealing (SA); its variant, an improved nonequilibrium simulated annealing (I-NESA); and the fuzzy global optimization (FO). The results showed that the GM is not superior but very challenging with the other applied methods. Agarwal and Sharma [16] used the basic ant colony optimization, including an adaptive penalty function, to handle the design constraints (ASACO) and the results obtained were compared to those obtained by the genetic algorithms (GAs) with a dynamic adaptive penalty strategy proposed in Ref. [17]. Zou et al. [18] proposed a novel modified differential evolution (NMDE). The NMDE was tested on the ROPs of the complex (bridge) and the overspeed protection systems. The results obtained showed that in each problem, the NMDE is superior to three other solution approaches available in the literature. Garg [19] used the cuckoo search (CS) with a penalty function. It was tested over 25 independent runs in solving various ROPs and the results were promising compared to several works available in the literature. Mellal and Zio [20] proposed a penalty-guided stochastic fractal search (PSFS) for solving the three methods of system reliability optimization. Ten case studies were solved using the PSFS and the results obtained were better than those of 36 methods applied in the literature. Also, in Ref. [21], the PSFS showed its superiority over the GA and the cuckoo optimization algorithm with penalty function (PFCOA) in solving the reliability optimization of a system containing 30 subsystems connected in series. Mellal and Williams [22] implemented the GA, particle swarm optimization (PSO), and the cuckoo optimization algorithm (COA) to solve a system involving 20 subsystems in series. The COA has outperformed the GA and the PSO. Mellal and Zio [23] proposed an adaptive particle swarm optimization (ADAP-PSO) to consider the system reliability, cost, weight, and volume as objectives. The multiobjective optimization problem has been converted to a single-objective problem using a weighted sum method. The results showed that the ADAP-PSO performs better than the PSO. Taghiyeh et al. [24] considered the parameter uncertainties in the ROPs using fuzzy number theories. Sharma [25] proposed a bidirectional butterfly optimization algorithm (BBOA) and showed that it performs better than the BOA. In Refs. [1, 2, 26, 27], the authors addressed the ROPs with the cold-standby strategy using the integer programming [1], GAs [26], SFS [27], and enhanced nest cuckoo optimization algorithm (ENCOA) [2].

Dobani et al. [28] proposed using heterogeneous redundant components in the ROPs. It has been proven that this strategy increases the system reliability compared to systems with homogeneous components. A hybrid solution approach based on the SFS and the GA (SFS-GA) was proposed to solve the problem. Mellal et al. [29] proposed a hosted cuckoo optimization algorithm (HO-COA) to solve this type of ROP more effectively. The results showed that the HO-COA performs better than the SFS-GA, COA, differential evolution (DE), and flower pollination algorithm (FPA). Ouyang et al. [30] addressed a mixed redundancy strategy (active and cold-standby redundant components) with heterogeneous components and solved the problem using the PSO with stochastic perturbation nature (SPPSO). The results showed that this strategy reaches better reliability than the mixed redundancy strategy with homogeneous components. Table 1 summarizes the works reviewed in this section.

Table 1 **Summary of the listed previous works.**

Reference	Method	Reliability allocation	Redundancy allocation	Reliability-redundancy allocation	Strategy
[5]	Dynamic programming		X		Active, homogeneous components
[6]	Integer programming		X		Active, homogeneous components
[7]	Computational procedure		X		Active, homogeneous components
[15]	Genetic algorithms with evolutionary strategies (GMs)	X	X		Active, homogeneous components
[16]	Ant colony optimization with an adaptive penalty function (ASACO)		X		Active, homogeneous components
[17]	Genetic algorithms with dynamic adaptive penalty strategy (GAs)		X		Active, homogeneous components
[18]	Novel modified differential evolution (NMDE)			X	Active, homogeneous components
[19]	Cuckoo search with a penalty function (CS)		X	X	Active, homogeneous components
[20]	Penalty-guided stochastic fractal search (PSFS)	X	X	X	Active, homogeneous components

Continued

Table 1 Summary of the listed previous works—cont'd

Reference	Method	Reliability allocation	Redundancy allocation	Reliability-redundancy allocation	Strategy
[21]	Penalty-guided stochastic fractal search (PSFS)			X	Active, homogeneous components
[22]	Cuckoo optimization algorithm (COA)			X	Active, homogeneous components
[23]	Adaptive particle swarm optimization (ADAP-PSO)	X		X	Active, homogeneous components
[24]	α-level cuts			X	Active, homogeneous components
[25]	Bidirectional butterfly optimization algorithm (BBOA)		X	X	Active, homogeneous components
[1]	Integer programming		X		Cold-standby, homogeneous components
[2]	Enhanced nest cuckoo optimization algorithm (ENCOA)			X	Cold-standby, homogeneous components
[26]	Modified version of the genetic algorithm (GA)			X	Cold-standby, homogeneous components
[27]	Penalty-guided fractal search algorithm (SFS)			X	Cold-standby, homogeneous components
[28]	Hybrid stochastic fractal search with genetic algorithms (hSFS-GA)			X	Active, heterogeneous components
[29]	Hosted cuckoo optimization algorithm (HO-COA)			X	Active, heterogeneous components
[30]	Particle swarm optimization with stochastic perturbation nature (SPPSO)			X	Mixed, heterogeneous components

3. Problem description

The overspeed protection system contains mechanical and electrical systems that protect the gas turbine in the power plant. It involves 4-stage control valves (V1–V4) connected in series (see Fig. 1, [20, 31–33]). The reliability-redundancy allocation problem was initially described by Dhingra [34]:

$$\text{Maximize } R_s(r, n) = \prod_{i=1}^{4} [1 - (1 - r_i)^{n_i}] \tag{1}$$

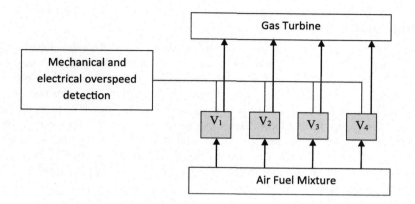

FIG. 1

Overspeed protection system.

subject to

$$R_s(r, n) \geq R \tag{2}$$

$$g_1(r, n) = \sum_{i=1}^{4} v_i n_i^2 \leq V \tag{3}$$

$$g_2(r, n) = \sum_{i=1}^{4} \tau_i (-T/\ln r_i)^{\varsigma_i} [n_i + \exp(n_i/4)] \leq C \tag{4}$$

$$g_3(r, n) = \sum_{i=1}^{4} w_i n_i \exp(n_i/4) \leq W \tag{5}$$

$$0.5 \leq r_i \leq 1 - 10^{-6}, \ 1 \leq n_i \leq 10, \ n_i \in \mathbb{Z}^+; \ i = 1, 2, \ldots, 4 \tag{6}$$

where $R_s(r,n)$ is the reliability of the overspeed protection system, r is the vector of the control valves' reliabilities, n is the vector of the number of redundant control valves, r_i is the reliability of the control valve at stage i, n_i is the number of redundant control valves at stage i, τ and ζ are the physical characteristics of each control valve at each stage, T is the mission time, v_i is the volume of each control valve at stage i, w_i is the weight of each control valve at stage i, R is the minimum allowable system reliability, V is the maximum allowable volume, C is the maximum cost, and W is the maximum weight. Table 2 reports the data of the system, where the cost, volume, and weight are given in arbitrary units.

Stage i	$10^5 \sigma_i$	ς_i	v_i	w_i	V	C	W	R	T (h)
1	1.0	1.5	1	6	250	400	500	0.75	1000
2	2.3	1.5	2	6					
3	0.3	1.5	3	8					
4	2.3	1.5	2	7					

Table 2 Data of the system.

4. Grey wolf optimizer

The grey wolf optimizer (GWO) is a nature-inspired optimization algorithm developed in 2014 by Mirjalili et al. [35], inspired by the lifestyle of grey wolves. This species of wolf lives in groups of 5–12 individuals and has four hierarchies: α, β, δ, and ω. The leader, Alpha (α), could be male or female and is mainly responsible for decision-making regarding hunting, resting place, etc. The individual Betas (β) are the second level of hierarchy. They help the leader to make decisions or to perform other activities as part of the group. Like Alphas, Betas can be male or female. They are probably the best candidates to replace the leader in case the Alpha wolf dies or gets very old. The Deltas (δ) warn the pack of wolves in case of danger, monitor the boundaries of the territory, etc. The Omegas (ω) are the weakest wolves and are subject to the other individuals. They are in the pack to maintain the diversity of the population.

The hunt follows three main steps:

- Search for prey.
- Surround the prey and attack.
- Perform optimization.

The mathematical principles of the GWO and its applications can be found in Refs. [35, 36]. The pseudocode of the implemented GWO is illustrated in Algorithm 1.

Algorithm 1 Pseudocode of the implemented GWO [35].

> Initialize the population of the grey wolves;
> Initialize α, β, and δ;
> Compute the fitness of each search agent and constraint handling;
> **While** (number of iterations $\leq$ maximum number of iterations) **do**
> > **For** each search agent
> > > Update the position of the current search position;
> >
> > **End for**
> > Update α, β, and δ;
> > Compute the fitness of all search agents and constraint handling;
> > Update the best agents α, β, and δ;
>
> **End while**
> Display the results.

5. Shuffled frog-leaping algorithm

The shuffled frog-leaping algorithm (SFLA) is a nature-inspired optimization algorithm proposed by Eusuff et al. in 2006 [37]. It is inspired by the lifestyle of frogs in terms of leaping and finding food. In this optimization algorithm, the frog population is divided into different groups called memeplexes. In each group, the behavior of each frog can be affected by other frogs. The SFLA was initially developed to solve combinatorial optimization problems. It combines the advantages of the memetic algorithm

(MA) [38] and PSO [39]. Detailed principles of the SFLA can be found in Refs. [37, 40]. Algorithm 2 illustrates the pseudocode of the implemented SFLA.

Algorithm 2 Pseudocode of the implemented SFLA [37].

Generate a random population;
Evaluate the fitness and constraint handling;
Find the physical form of the population;
Sort the members (frogs) by performance;
While (number of iterations ≤ maximum number of iterations) **do.**
    Separate the frogs in groups (memeplexes);
    Evaluate each memeplex and constraint handling;
    Generate a submemeplex from the current memeplex;
    Find the worst frog position;
    Update the worst frog position;
    Sort the memeplexes by performance;
    Mix the memeplexes and sort the population;
    Update the best results;

End while
Display the results.

6. Results and discussion

The GWO and the SFLA were implemented using MATLAB 2017a and run over 10 independent executions on a personal computer with the following characteristics: i3 M380 processor with 2.53 GHz, 4 GB of RAM, and Windows 7 with 64 bits. The design constraints were handled using penalty functions. The population size is 500 and the maximum number of iterations is 1000. The best reliability value R_s, the number of function evaluations needed to reach the optimal solution (NFE), CPU time, and the standard deviation (σ) are used as performance metrics to compare the performances of the optimization algorithm in solving the described problem.

From Table 3, it can be observed that the best system reliability value obtained by the GWO is 0.99995465911 at run #3. The CPU time is 2.61 s, the NFE is 100,000, and the value of σ is 4.663845E − 06. Table 4 reports that the best system reliability value obtained by the SFLA is at run #9 (R_s = 0.99995467466; CPU = 74.04 s; NFE = 98,500; σ = 5.051297E − 06). The results and performance comparisons are reported in Table 5 and illustrated in Figs. 2–5. It can be observed that the SFLA provided a better system reliability value and used fewer NFEs than the GWO. However, it consumed more CPU time and has a greater standard deviation.

7. Conclusions

This chapter illustrated the reliability-redundancy optimization problem of the overspeed protection system of the gas turbine in the power plant. The system consists of four control valves connected in series. The objective was to maximize the system reliability under the minimum allowable reliability

Table 3 Results obtained by GWO.

No	(n_1, n_2, n_3, n_4)	r_1	r_2	r_3	r_4	R_s	CPU (s)	NFE	σ
1	(5, 5, 4, 6)	0.900538	0.887970	0.948363	0.851154	0.9999463573	2.61	100,000	4.663845E−06
2	(5, 5, 4, 6)	0.901412	0.887837	0.948545	0.850277	0.99995465523	2.48	100,000	
3	(5, 6, 4, 5)	0.901917	0.849050	0.948102	0.888570	**0.99995465911**	2.61	100,000	
4	(5, 5, 4, 6)	0.902527	0.888426	0.947300	0.849612	0.9999545462923	2.33	100,000	
5	(5, 5, 4, 6)	0.901134	0.888492	0.948826	0.849068	0.99995463515	2.93	100,000	
6	(4, 6, 5, 5)	0.932964	0.845554	0.914741	0.883942	0.9999467403	2.23	100,000	
7	(6, 5, 4, 5)	0.863253	0.884723	0.947629	0.885710	0.9999608247	2.27	100,000	
8	(5, 6, 4, 5)	0.901086	0.850792	0.948462	0.887788	0.99995465135	2.37	100,000	
9	(5, 5, 4, 6)	0.902528	0.888413	0.947145	0.849811	0.99995462005	2.16	100,000	
10	(5, 5, 4, 6)	0.901827	0.887925	0.949187	0.848889	0.9999546262	2.22	100,000	

Table 4 Results obtained by SFLA.

No	(n_1, n_2, n_3, n_4)	r_1	r_2	r_3	r_4	R_s	CPU (s)	NFE	σ
1	(4, 5, 5, 6)	0.932745	0.884220	0.915347	0.845319	0.9999409260	45.51	93,000	5.051297E−06
2	(6, 5, 4, 5)	0.862917	0.885617	0.946748	0.885585	0.99994613666	61.20	93,500	
3	(5, 5, 4, 6)	0.901623	0.888282	0.948078	0.849888	0.99995467445	65.72	86,500	
4	(6, 5, 4, 5)	0.862830	0.885663	0.946752	0.885565	0.99994613650	65.04	94,000	
5	(5, 5, 5, 5)	0.899162	0.885452	0.916123	0.885650	0.99994615053	63.91	75,000	
6	(5, 5, 4, 6)	0.901627	0.888215	0.948158	0.849901	0.99995467464	72.70	92,000	
7	(5, 6, 4, 5)	0.901604	0.850038	0.948029	0.888239	0.99995467403	75.40	99,000	
8	(5, 6, 4, 5)	0.901625	0.849936	0.948174	0.888183	0.99995467460	80.00	85,000	
9	(5, 5, 4, 6)	0.901592	0.888234	0.948144	0.849919	**0.99995467466**	74.04	98,500	
10	(5, 5, 5, 5)	0.899246	0.885492	0.916240	0.885525	0.99994615443	74.62	93,500	

Table 5 Comparison of GWO vs. SFLA.				
	R_s	NFE	CPU	σ
GWO	0.99995465911	100,000	**2.61**	**4.663845E − 06**
SFLA	**0.99995467466**	**98,500**	74.04	5.051297E − 06

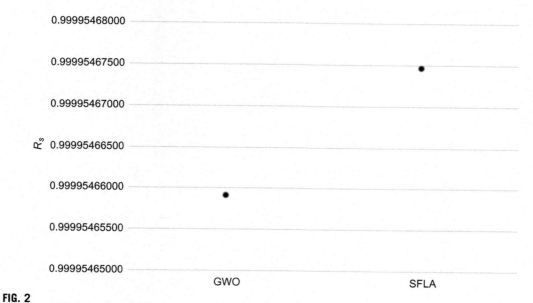

FIG. 2

Best reliability obtained by GWO and SFLA.

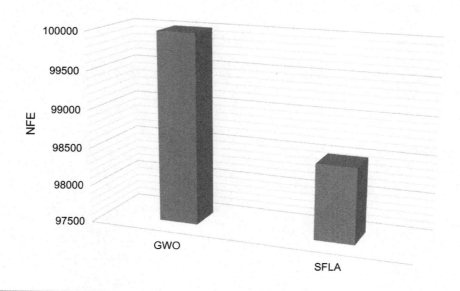

FIG. 3

NFE used by GWO and SFLA.

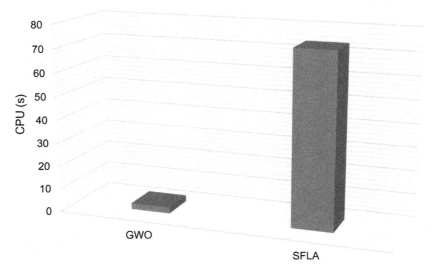

FIG. 4

CPU consumed by GWO and SFLA.

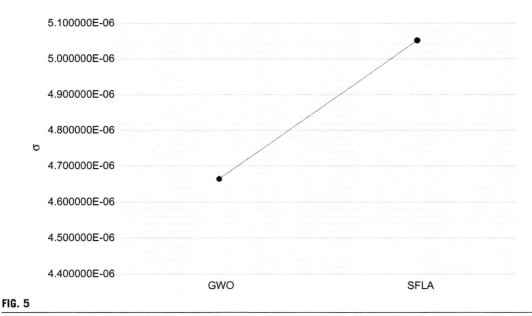

FIG. 5

Standard deviation of GWO and SFLA.

value and the limits of cost, weight, and volume. The GWO and the SFLA with penalty functions were implemented to solve the problem. The results revealed that the SFLA provides a better system reliability and used fewer NFEs but consumed a higher CPU time and has a much worse standard deviation than the GWO. Future works will focus on the multicriteria problem of this system using the multi-objective versions of these optimization algorithms.

References

[1] D.W. Coit, Cold-standby redundancy optimization for nonrepairable systems, IIE Trans. 33 (2001) 471–478.

[2] M.A. Mellal, E. Zio, System reliability-redundancy optimization with cold-standby strategy by an enhanced nest cuckoo optimization algorithm, Reliab. Eng. Syst. Saf. 201 (2020) 106973.

[3] K.C. Kapur, M. Pecht, Reliability engineering, John Wiley & Sons, Inc., Hoboken, NJ, USA, 2014.

[4] E. Zio, An introduction to the basics of reliability and risk analysis, thirteenth ed., World Scientific, Singapore, 2007.

[5] R. Bellman, S. Dreyfus, Dynamic programming and the reliability of multicomponent devices, Oper. Res. 6 (1958) 200–206.

[6] F.A. Tillman, J.M. Liittschwager, Integer programming formulation of constrained reliability problems, Manag. Sci. 13 (1967) 887–899.

[7] F.A. Tillman, C.L. Hwang, L.T. Fan, S.A. Balbale, Systems reliability subject to multiple nonlinear constraints, IEEE Trans. Reliab. R-17 (1968) 153–157, https://doi.org/10.1109/TR.1968.5216929.

[8] M.A. Mellal, Soft computing methods for system dependability, IGI Global, USA, 2020.

[9] M.A. Mellal, A. Salhi, Parallel-series system optimization by weighting sum methods and nature-inspired computing, in: Applied Nature-Inspired Computing: Algorithms and Case Studies, Springer, 2020, https://doi.org/10.1007/978-981-13-9263-4_10.

[10] M.A. Mellal, E.J. Williams, A survey on ant colony optimization, particle swarm optimization, and cuckoo algorithms, in: P. Samui, S. Sekhar, V.E. Balas (Eds.), Handbook of Research on Emergent Applications of Optimization Algorithms, IGI Global, 2018, pp. 37–51.

[11] M.A. Mellal, E.J. Williams, The cuckoo optimization algorithm and its applications, in: Handbook of Neural Computation, Elsevier, 2017, pp. 269–277.

[12] M.A. Mellal, M. Pecht, A multi-objective design optimization framework for wind turbines under altitude consideration, Energ. Conver. Manage. 222 (2020) 113212, https://doi.org/10.1016/j.enconman.2020.113212.

[13] W. Kuo, R. Wan, Recent advances in optimal reliability allocation, in: G. Levitin (Ed.), Computational Intelligence in Reliability Engineering, Springer, Berlin, Germany, 2007, pp. 1–36.

[14] W. Kuo, R. Wan, Recent advances in optimal reliability allocation, IEEE Trans. Syst. Man Cybern. Part A Syst. Hum. 37 (2007) 143–156, https://doi.org/10.1109/TSMCA.2006.889476.

[15] F. Bicking, Allocation de la fiabilité par algorithme génétique: application à la conception d'un Système Instrumenté de Sécurité, J. Natl. La Rech. En IUT (2009) 30–52.

[16] M. Agarwal, V.K. Sharma, Ant colony approach to constrained redundancy optimization in binary systems, App. Math. Model. 34 (2010) 992–1003, https://doi.org/10.1016/j.apm.2009.07.016.

[17] M. Agarwal, R. Gupta, Genetic search for redundancy optimization in complex systems, J. Qual. Maint. Eng. 12 (2006) 338–353, https://doi.org/10.1108/13552510610705919.

[18] D. Zou, H. Liu, L. Gao, S. Li, A novel modified differential evolution algorithm for constrained optimization problems, Comput. Math. Appl. 61 (2011) 1608–1623, https://doi.org/10.1016/j.camwa.2011.01.029.

[19] H. Garg, An approach for solving constrained reliability-redundancy allocation problems using cuckoo search algorithm, Beni-Suef Univ. J. Basic Appl. Sci. 4 (2015) 14–25, https://doi.org/10.1016/j.bjbas.2015.02.003.

[20] M.A. Mellal, E. Zio, A penalty guided stochastic fractal search approach for system reliability optimization, Reliab. Eng. Syst. Saf. 152 (2016) 213–227.

[21] M.A. Mellal, E. Zio, System reliability-redundancy allocation by evolutionary computation, in: Proceedings of the 2nd International Conference on System Reliability and Safety (ICSRS), IEEE, Milan, Italy, 2017, pp. 15–19.

[22] M.A. Mellal, E.J. Williams, Large scale reliability-redundancy allocation optimization problem using three soft computing methods, in: Modeling and Simulation Based Analysis in Reliability Engineering, CRC Press Francis & Taylor, 2018, pp. 199–214.

[23] M.A. Mellal, E. Zio, An adaptive particle swarm optimization method for multi-objective system reliability optimization, J. Risk Reliab. 233 (2019) 990–1001, https://doi.org/10.1177/1748006X19852814.

[24] S. Taghiyeh, M. Mahmoudi, S. Fadaie, H. Tohidi, Fuzzy reliability-redundancy allocation problem of the overspeed protection system, Eng. Rep. 2 (2020), https://doi.org/10.1002/eng2.12221.

[25] T.K. Sharma, Enhanced butterfly optimization algorithm for reliability optimization problems, J. Ambient. Intell. Humaniz. Comput. 1 (2020) 3, https://doi.org/10.1007/s12652-020-02481-2.

[26] M.A. Ardakan, A.Z. Hamadani, Reliability-redundancy allocation problem with cold-standby redundancy strategy, Simul. Model. Pract. Theory 42 (2014) 107–118.

[27] M.N. Juybari, M. Abouei Ardakan, H. Davari-Ardakani, A penalty-guided fractal search algorithm for reliability–redundancy allocation problems with cold-standby strategy, Proc. Inst. Mech. Eng. Part O J. Risk Reliab. (2019), https://doi.org/10.1177/1748006X19825707.

[28] E.R. Dobani, M.A. Ardakan, H. Davari-Ardakani, M.N. Juybari, RRAP-CM: a new reliability-redundancy allocation problem with heterogeneous components, Reliab. Eng. Syst. Saf. (2019), https://doi.org/10.1016/j.ress.2019.106563.

[29] M.A. Mellal, S. Al-Dahidi, E.J. Williams, System reliability optimization with heterogeneous components using hosted cuckoo optimization algorithm, Reliab. Eng. Syst. Saf. 203 (2020) 107110, https://doi.org/10.1016/j.ress.2020.107110.

[30] Z. Ouyang, Y. Liu, S.J. Ruan, T. Jiang, An improved particle swarm optimization algorithm for reliability-redundancy allocation problem with mixed redundancy strategy and heterogeneous components, Reliab. Eng. Syst. Saf. 181 (2019) 62–74.

[31] B.N. Chebouba, M.A. Mellal, S. Adjerid, D. Benazzouz, System reliability and cost optimization under various scenarios using NSGA-III, in: 2020 International Conference on Electrical Engineering, ICEE, 2020, pp. 1–6, https://doi.org/10.1109/ICEE49691.2020.9249929.

[32] B.N. Chebouba, M.A. Mellal, S. Adjerid, Multi-objective system reliability optimization in a power plant, in: 2018 International Conference on Electrical Sciences and Technologies in Maghreb, 2018, pp. 1–4, https://doi.org/10.1109/CISTEM.2018.8613549.

[33] M.A. Mellal, B.N. Chebouba, Cost and availability optimization of Overspeed protection system in a power plant, in: 2019 International Conference on Advanced Electrical Engineering, 2019, pp. 1–4, https://doi.org/10.1109/ICAEE47123.2019.9015115.

[34] A.K. Dhingra, Optimal apportionment of reliability and redundancy in series systems under multiple objectives, IEEE Trans. Reliab. 41 (1992) 576–582, https://doi.org/10.1109/24.249589.

[35] S. Mirjalili, S.M. Mirjalili, A. Lewis, Grey wolf optimizer, Adv. Eng. Softw. 69 (2014) 46–61, https://doi.org/10.1016/j.advengsoft.2013.12.007.

[36] M. Panda, B. Das, Grey wolf optimizer and its applications: a survey, in: Lecture Notes in Electrical Engineering, Springer Verlag, 2019, pp. 179–194, https://doi.org/10.1007/978-981-13-7091-5_17.

[37] M. Eusuff, K. Lansey, F. Pasha, Shuffled frog-leaping algorithm: a memetic meta-heuristic for discrete optimization, Eng. Optim. 38 (2006) 129–154.

[38] P. Moscato, On evolution, search, optimization, genetic algorithms and martial arts: Towards memetic algorithms, California Institute of Technology, CA, USA, 1989.

[39] J. Kennedy, R. Eberhart, Particle swarm optimization, in: Proceedings of the IEEE International Conference on Neural Networks, vol. 4, 1995, pp. 1942–1948, https://doi.org/10.1109/ICNN.1995.488968.

[40] B.G. Rajeev Gandhi, R.K. Bhattacharjya, Introduction to shuffled frog leaping algorithm and its sensitivity to the parameters of the algorithm, in: F. Bennis, R.K. Bhattacharjya (Eds.), Nature-Inspired Methods Metaheuristics Optimization, Springer, 2020, pp. 105–117.

Design optimization of a car side safety system by particle swarm optimization and grey wolf optimizer

Ikram Hamadache[a] **and Mohamed Arezki Mellal**[a,b]

LMSS, Faculty of Technology, M'Hamed Bougara University, Boumerdes, Algeria[a] *Center for Advanced Life Cycle Engineering (CALCE), University of Maryland, College Park, MD, United States*[b]

1. Introduction

Nowadays, the significant use of utility products, such as automobiles, pressures the industrial companies to satisfy the consumers due to public safety, regulations, and competitiveness. To meet these requirements, manufacturers must mobilize their efforts [1–3]. On the other hand, the world is witnessing a great technological development regarding automobiles, and this technology is mainly made after using optimization methods (maximizing or minimizing a single function or multiple functions). In this context, manufacturers must optimize automobile parts, whose goal is to have a better-required function of the automobile, i.e., to give more satisfaction to the customers, e.g., braking system, steering system, comfort, design, aerodynamics, and safe structure.

The most important concern for automobile users is safety. To achieve a high safety level, industrial manufactures have optimized different parts and systems of automobiles. Most of the solution approaches were based on computational intelligence methods due to their many advantages [4–7]. Yildiz [8] proposed a new hybrid approach combining the artificial immune algorithm and Taguchi's method to optimize the shape of automobile parts. In [9], the structure design of a vehicle part has been optimized using particle swarm optimization combined with Taguchi's method, whereas in [10] the same problem has been solved using the cuckoo search algorithm. Li et al. [11] used genetic algorithms to optimize the restraint system for safety maximization.

In this chapter, the design of a car side safety system is optimized using two optimization techniques, namely, particle swarm optimization (PSO) and the grey wolf optimizer (GWO). It is organized as follows: Section 2 describes the problem. Sections 3 and 4 give an overview of the principles of PSO and GWO. The results obtained with a discussion are given in Section 5. Finally, the last section concludes this chapter with some remarks and future directions.

2. Design optimization of a car side safety system

The objective of this optimization problem is to minimize the weight of the car side safety system (see Fig. 1). There is a barrier in the door for structural reinforcement. The problem involves 11 decision variables, including two variables given in a set for choosing the materials (mild steel MS or high-strength steel), and subject to 21 design constraints. Therefore, the problem is hard to solve and needs efficient solution techniques. It is formulated as follows [12,13]:

$$\text{Weight}(x) = 1.98 + 4.90x_1 + 6.67x_2 + 6.98x_3 + 4.01x_4 + 1.78x_5 + 2.73x_7 \ (\text{kg}) \tag{1}$$

subject to

$$0.5 \le x_1, x_2, x_3, x_4, x_5, x_6, x_7 \le 1.5 \tag{2}$$

$$x_8, x_9 \in \{0.192, 0.345\} \tag{3}$$

$$-30\,\text{mm} \le x_{10}, x_{11} \le 30\,\text{mm} \tag{4}$$

$$g_1 : F_{Abdom} = 1.16 - 0.003717x_2x_4 - 0.00931x_2x_{10} - 0.484x_3x_9 + 0.01343x_6x_{10} \le 1\,\text{kN} \tag{5}$$

FIG. 1

Car side safety system.

$$g_2 : VC_{upper} = 0.261 - 0.0159x_1x_2 - 0.188x_1x_8 - 0.019x_2x_7 + 0.0144x_3x_5$$
$$+ 0.0008757x_5x_{10} + 0.08045x_6x_9 + 0.00139x_8x_{11} + 0.00001575x_{10}x_{11} \le 0.32\,\text{m/s} \tag{6}$$

$$g_3 : VC_{middle} = 0.214 + 0.00817x_5 - 0.131x_1x_8 - 0.0704x_1x_9 + 0.03099x_2x_6$$
$$- 0.018x_2x_7 + 0.0208x_3x_8 + 0.121x_3x_9 - 0.00364x_5x_6$$
$$+ 0.0007715x_5x_{10} - 0.0005354x_6x_{10} + 0.00121x_8x_{11} \le 0.32\,\text{m/s} \tag{7}$$

$$g_4 : VC_{lower} = 0.74 - 0.61x_2 - 0.163x_3x_8 + 0.001232x_3x_{10} - 0.166x_7x_9 + 0.227x_2^2 \le 0.32\,\text{m/s} \tag{8}$$

$$g_5 : Def_{rib\_upper} = 28.98 + 3.818x_3 - 4.2x_1x_2 + 0.0207x_5x_{10} + 6.63x_6x_9 - 7.7x_7x_8$$
$$+ 0.32x_9x_{10} \le 32\,\text{mm} \tag{9}$$

$$g_6 : Def_{rib\_middle} = 33.86 + 2.95x_3 + 0.1792x_{10} - 5.057x_1x_2 - 11.0x_2x_8$$
$$- 0.0215x_5x_{10} - 9.98x_7x_8 + 22.0x_8x_9 \le 32\,\text{mm} \tag{10}$$

$$g_7 : Def_{rib\_lower} = 46.36 - 9.9x_2 - 12.9x_1x_8 + 0.1107x_3x_{10} \le 32\,\text{mm} \tag{11}$$

$$g_8 : F_{Pubic} = 4.72 - 0.5x_4 - 0.19x_2x_3 - 0.0122x_4x_{10} + 0.09325x_6x_{10} + 0.000191x_{11}^2 \le 4\,\text{kN} \tag{12}$$

$$g_9 : V_{B-Pillar} = 10.58 - 0.674x_1x_2 - 1.95x_2x_8 + 0.02054x_3x_{10} - 0.0198x_4x_{10}$$
$$+ 0.028x_6x_{10} \le 9.9\,\text{mm/ms} \tag{13}$$

$$g_{10} : V_{Front\,door} = 16.45 - 0.489x_3x_7 - 0.843x_5x_6 + 0.0432x_9x_{10} - 0.0556x_9x_{11}$$
$$- 0.000786x_{11}^2 \le 15.7\,\text{mm/ms} \tag{14}$$

where x_1 is the thickness of the B-pillar inner, x_2 is the thickness of the B-pillar reinforcement, x_3 is the thickness of the inner floor side, x_4 is the thickness of cross members, x_5 is the thickness of the door beam, x_6 is the thickness of the door belt line reinforcement, x_7 is the thickness of the roof rail, x_8 is the material of the B-pillar inner, x_9 is the material of the inner floor side, x_{10} is the barrier height, x_{11} is the barrier hitting position, F_{Abdom} is the abdomen force, VC is the viscous criterion, Def_{rib} is the rib deflection, F_{Pubic} is the pubic symphysis force, $V_{B-Pillar}$ is the velocity of the B-pillar at the middle point, and $V_{Front\,door}$ is the velocity of the front door at the B-pillar.

3. Particle swarm optimization

The particle swarm optimization (PSO) algorithm has been developed in 1995 by Kennedy and Eberhant [14]. It inspired by the behavior of animals and insects that live in swarms, e.g., birds and fish. In order to find the best food regions, each individual keeps his personal memory of the experience as well as all the information provided by his group. This individual is called particle i. More details on the principles of the PSO can be found in Refs. [14–18]. The pseudocode of the implemented PSO is illustrated in Algorithm 1.

Algorithm 1 Pseudocode of the implemented PSO.

> Put of the parameters;
> Initialization;
> **While** number of iterations not reached.
>> Objective function evaluation;
>> Constraint handling using penalty function;
>> Velocity of each particle;
>> Best particle;
>> Update positions;
>
> **End while.**
> Display the results.

4. Grey wolf optimizer

The grey wolf optimizer (GWO) has been proposed by Mirjalili et al. in 2014 [19]. It is inspired by the grey wolf hunting strategy. The GWO process is simulated at the leadership hierarchy. In the wolf pack, the leader can be male or female who is called Alpha (α) and the sub-leaders are the Beta (β). The task of the beta wolf is to help the leaders (Alpha) to make decisions. If the alpha wolves die or age, the beta will replace them (to make the decisions). The last wolves in the hierarchical classification are called Omega (ω). They cannot eat without permission from the chefs. The other wolves are called the sub-ordinates or Delta (δ) and are ranked third in the hierarchy of wolves. More details on the GWO can found in Refs. [19–22]. Algorithm 2 illustrates the pseudocode of the implemented GWO.

Algorithm 2 Pseudocode of the implemented GWO.

> Put of the parameters;
> Initialize the grey wolf population;
> Calculate the suitability of each research agent;
> $X_\alpha =$ best search agent;
> $X_\beta =$ second best search agent;
> $X_\delta =$ third best search agent;
> **While** number of iterations not reached
>> **For** each search agent
>> Update current search agent position;
>> **End for**
>> Update*s;*
>> Calculate the suitability of each research agent;
>> Constraint handling using penalty functions;
>> Updates;
>
> **End while**
> Display the results.

5. Results and discussion

The two optimization algorithms have been implemented using MATLAB R2017a and executed on a PC with the following characteristics: Intel (R) Core (TM) i5-3230M CPU, 4 GB of RAM with a 64-bit operating system. The design constraints are handled using penalty functions. The population size and number of iterations are 100 and 1000, respectively. These parameters have been fixed after trial-and-error and each algorithm has been run over 10 independent runs.

Tables 1–3 report the results obtained with the PSO. The minimum weight, number of function evaluations (NFEs), CPU time, and standard deviation (SD) are given in Table 3. The best results are highlighted in bold type. The minimum weight has been obtained at the first run (22.847423 kg) with 93,400 of NFE, 395.734690 s of CPU, and the SD is 0.4546. Fig. 2 shows the convergence for the minimum weight.

Tables 4–6 report the results obtained using the GWO. Table 4 reveals that the minimum weight has been obtained at the third run with 22.848258 kg. The NFE is 96,800, the CPU is 391.518399 s, and the standard deviation is 0.4994. The decision variables and constraints are given in Tables 5 and 6, respectively. The convergence of the best result is shown in Fig. 3.

The performances of the PSO and the GWO in solving the optimization problem of the car side safety system are reported in Table 7. It can be observed that the PSO has outperformed the GWO in terms of better weight, number of function evaluations, and standard deviation. However, GWO performs faster.

Table 1 Results of 10 runs using PSO.

No	Weight (kg)	NFE	CPU (s)	σ
1	**22.847423**	93,400	395.734690	0.4546
2	22.862527	99,700	399.619837	
3	23.313472	98,100	368.309252	
4	22,880,062	98,200	382.400233	
5	22.864014	99,300	390.893768	
6	22.856085	93,500	378.534450	
7	22.854419	100,000	376.637470	
8	23.333234	99,700	380.762643	
9	22.848841	87,100	378.208781	
10	22.852899	98,200	384.943814	

Table 2 Design variables using PSO.

No	x_1	x_2	x_3	x_4	x_5	x_6	x_7	x_8	x_9	$3x_{10}$	x_{11}
1	0.500000	1.125132	0.503634	1.305730	0.500000	1.488970	0.516813	0.192	0.345	−18.365846	3.646460
2	0.537211	1.106172	0.500000	1.563432	0.632946	0.647633	0.505613	0.3450	0.1920	4.991835	14.069876
3	0.500000	1.211763	0.500000	1.223422	0.500000	1.500000	0.508901	0.3450	0.3450	−2.700634	2.947350
4	0.504918	1.278599	0.500000	1.225373	0.512052	1.394873	0.506547	0.3450	0.1920	9.743396	12.804624
5	0.500544	1.118166	0.506228	1.342018	0.503382	1.491187	0.511404	0.3450	0.3450	−19.717543	5.921798
6	0.505634	1.086706	0.505740	1.391542	0.503988	1.500000	0.501369	0.3450	0.3450	−24.89322	−4.419210
7	0.509268	1.136694	0.500467	1.281590	0.509771	1.500000	0.505938	0.3450	0.1920	−16.307905	1.682262
8	0.544540	1.181371	0.500000	1.302137	0.500000	1.422607	0.500000	0.3450	0.1920	−4.905455	12.454555
9	0.511669	1.204609	0.500000	1.361725	0.516728	0.512861	0.500000	0.3450	0.3450	−3.198793	13.835946
10	0.500000	1.148389	0.500000	1.270063	0.505537	1.487298	0.504022	0.3450	0.3450	−14.554991	0.057300

Table 3 Results of the constraints using PSO.

No	g_1	g_2	g_3	g_4	g_5	g_6	g_7	g_8	g_9	g_{10}
1	0.349538	0.260794	0.263981	0.284668	28.939039	27.446204	31.945196	3.998907	9.282869	15.323499
2	0.537663	0.227970	0.222015	0.291266	27.954873	27.781515	31.889632	3.991081	9.311754	15.712135
3	0.497436	0.252211	0.252942	0.274066	30.054622	27.993421	31.3858224	3.997362	9.2677812	15.583520
4	0.589870	0.241823	0.247131	0.292580	28.619660	31.974950	31.3974950	3.990032	9.526718	15.543297
5	0.330498	0.246962	0.256725	0.271334	28.134299	25.699046	31.896412	4.00000	8.929916	15.257539
6	0.275952	0.241383	0.254321	0.271955	27.684953	25.143312	31.998974	4.00000	8.847290	15.379474
7	0.413087	0.227997	0.251025	0.284379	27.842489	25.017374	31.814760	3.996700	8.976562	15.527064
8	0.505069	0.232986	0.246805	0.288331	28.280752	26.454551	31.917446	4.00001	9.226076	15.433483
9	0.469492	0.229895	0.220471	0.275056	27.781348	27.981947	31.911837	3.990657	9.354400	15.629079
10	0.393161	0.246948	0.254180	0.271959	28.815202	26.47721	31.84924	3.993740	9.024046	15.466661

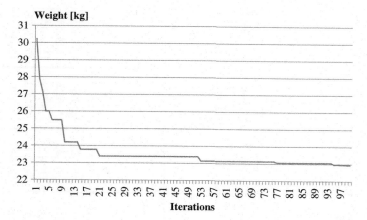

FIG. 2

Convergence of the minimum weight using PSO.

Table 4 Results of 10 runs using GWO.

No	Weight (kg)	NFE	CPU (s)	σ
1	22.976626	100,000	407.742169	0.4994
2	22.850683	100,000	407.979208	
3	**22.848258**	96,800	391.518399	
4	22.849348	100,000	367.570144	
5	23.323722	99,900	379.721893	
6	22.885656	100,000	373.389834	
7	23.343732	100,000	427.876858	
8	22.863860	99,900	390.233964	
9	22.862194	100,000	386.371885	
10	23.243814	100,000	363.994953	

6. Conclusions

In this chapter, two nature-inspired optimization algorithms, the particle swarm optimization (PSO) and the grey wolf optimizer (GWO), have been used to solve the design optimization of the car side safety system. The problem requires a strong constraint-handling method. The results obtained revealed that the PSO provided the minimum weight, required fewer functions of evaluations, and has less standard deviation than the GWO. However, this end is faster. The overall comparison shows that the PSO has outperformed the GWO. Future works will be devoted to the development of a hybrid nature-inspired optimization algorithm to reach better results.

Table 5 Design variables using GWO.

No	x_1	x_2	x_3	x_4	x_5	x_6	x_7	x_8	x_9	x_{10}	x_{11}
1	0.500000	1.173353	0.500000	1.240690	0.500098	1.499796	0.500005	0.3450	0.3450	-9.437397	2.157596
2	0.500069	1.111712	0.501047	1.309923	0.500068	1.499228	0.500000	0.3450	0.3450	-20.365376	-0.045168
3	0.500000	1.112055	0.500000	1.310684	0.500000	1.500000	0.500000	0.1920	0.3450	-20.404887	0.395053
4	0.500124	1.108476	0.500000	1.316516	0.500000	1.500000	0.500355	0.3450	0.1920	-20.979030	0.508812
5	0.500664	1.229801	0.500533	1.231336	0.500637	1.076042	0.500063	0.3450	0.3450	0.773582	9.254184
6	0.500151	1.111576	0.500000	1.320537	0.500193	1.500000	0.500000	0.3450	0.3450	-20.457450	3.434072
7	0.500167	1.240485	0.500245	1.219033	0.502155	0.947307	0.500000	0.3450	0.3450	2.607448	10.954347
8	0.500000	1.118300	0.500032	1.303189	0.500930	1.500000	0.500778	0.3450	0.1920	-19.227175	2.3033584
9	0.500754	1.110645	0.500267	1.314540	0.500485	1.499754	0.500533	0.3450	0.1920	-20.576898	-1.728459
10	0.500000	1.213072	0.500117	1.240832	0.500596	1.496750	0.500000	0.3450	0.1920	-2.416818	8.174094

Table 6 Results of the constraints using GWO.

No	g_1	g_2	g_3	g_4	g_5	g_6	g_7	g_8	g_9	g_{10}
1	0.447302	0.250112	0.253879	0.274091	29.381851	27.213855	31.983852	3.999191	9.133289	15.509914
2	0.335221	0.245265	0.255269	0.272847	28.190560	25.758879	31.984183	4.000000	8.918877	15.391771
3	0.335125	0.259826	0.263800	0.285452	28.781804	27.236641	32.00000	3.999927	9.251991	15.384136
4	0.364175	0.226960	0.251757	0.285622	27.634734	24.521334	31.987845	3.999492	8.910325	15.515583
5	0.515054	0.245203	0.239508	0.276655	29.523556	28.563650	31.973055	3.999929	9.347139	15.640153
6	0.330673	0.246927	0.256743	0.272881	28.181761	25.745970	31.980837	4.000000	8.921223	15.315478
7	0.517149	0.243173	0.235604	0.277376	29.435435	28.817672	31.990710	3.999518	9.359304	15.660255
8	0.385179	0.228424	0.252102	0.285720	27.739613	24.75723	31.991401	4.000000	8.941200	15.506445
9	0.369222	0.225962	0.250610	0.285779	27.657430	24.579396	31.999597	3.999812	8.918328	15.540575
10	0.532748	0.236979	0.250979	0.288517	28.745514	26.993127	31.991525	3.999930	9.288364	15.536264

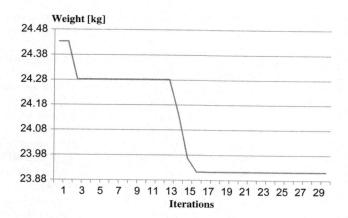

FIG. 3

Convergence of the minimum weight using GWO.

Table 7 Comparison of the performances (PSO vs. GWO).

Algorithm	Weight (kg)	CPU (s)	NFE	σ
GWO	22.848258	**391.518399**	96,800	0.4994
PSO	**22.847423**	395.734690	**93,400**	**0.4546**

References

[1] M.A. Mellal, Mechatronic Systems: Design, Performance and Applications, Nova Science Publishers, New York, USA, 2019. ISBN: 978-1-53614-530-4.

[2] M.A. Mellal, Manufacturing Systems: Recent Progress and Future Directions, Nova Science Publishers, New York, USA, 2020. ISBN: 978-1-53618-676-5.

[3] M.A. Mellal, Advanced Manufacturing: Progress, Trends and Challenges, Nova Science Publishers, New York, USA, 2020. ISBN: 978-1-53618-870-7.

[4] M.A. Mellal, Soft Computing Methods for System Dependability, IGI Global, USA, 2020. ISBN: 9781799817185.

[5] M.A. Mellal, E.J. Williams, The cuckoo optimization algorithm and its applications, in: Handbook of Neural Computation, Elsevier, 2017, pp. 269–277.

[6] M.A. Mellal, M. Pecht, A multi-objective design optimization framework for wind turbines under altitude consideration, Energ. Conver. Manage. 222 (2020) 113212, https://doi.org/10.1016/j.enconman.2020.113212.

[7] M.A. Mellal, A. Salhi, Parallel-series system optimization by weighting sum methods and nature-inspired computing, in: Applied Nature-Inspired Computing: Algorithms and Case Studies, Springer, 2020, https://doi.org/10.1007/978-981-13-9263-4_10.

[8] A.R. Yildiz, A new design optimization framework based on immune algorithm and Taguchi's method, Comput. Ind. (2009), https://doi.org/10.1016/j.compind.2009.05.016.

[9] A.R. Yildiz, A new hybrid particle swarm optimization approach for structural design optimization in the automotive industry, Proc. Inst. Mech. Eng. D J. Automob. Eng. 226 (2012) 1340–1351, https://doi.org/10.1177/0954407012443636.

[10] I. Durgun, A.R. Yildiz, Structural design optimization of vehicle components using cuckoo search algorithm, Mater. Test. 54 (2012) 185–188, https://doi.org/10.3139/120.110317.

[11] G. Li, Z. Xue, C.H. Chuang, K. Pline, Study of optimization strategy for vehicle restraint system design, in: SAE Technical Paper, SAE International, 2019, https://doi.org/10.4271/2019-01-1072.

[12] B.D. Youn, K.K. Choi, A new response surface methodology for reliability-based design optimization, Comput. Struct. 82 (2004) 241–256, https://doi.org/10.1016/j.compstruc.2003.09.002.

[13] L. Gu, R.J. Yang, C.H. Tho, M. Makowski, O. Faruque, Y. Li, Optimization and robustness for crashworthiness of side impact, Int. J. Veh. Des. 26 (2001) 348–360, https://doi.org/10.1504/IJVD.2001.005210.

[14] J. Kennedy, R. Eberhart, Particle swarm optimization, Neural Networks, in: Proceedings., IEEE Int. Conf. 4 (1995), vol.4, 1995, pp. 1942–1948, https://doi.org/10.1109/ICNN.1995.488968.

[15] J. Matos, R.P.V. Faria, I.B.R. Nogueira, J.M. Loureiro, A.M. Ribeiro, Optimization strategies for chiral separation by true moving bed chromatography using particles swarm optimization (PSO) and new parallel PSO variant, Comput. Chem. Eng. 123 (2019) 344–356, https://doi.org/10.1016/j.compchemeng.2019.01.020.

[16] M.A. Mellal, E. Zio, An adaptive particle swarm optimization method for multi-objective system reliability optimization, J. Risk Reliab. 233 (2019) 990–1001, https://doi.org/10.1177/1748006X19852814.

[17] M.A. Mellal, E.J. Williams, A survey on ant colony optimization, particle swarm optimization, and cuckoo algorithms, in: Handbook of Research on Emergent Applications of Optimization Algorithms, IGI Global, USA, 2018.

[18] N.K. Jain, U. Nangia, J. Jain, A review of particle swarm optimization, J. Inst. Eng. Ser. B. 99 (2018) 407–411, https://doi.org/10.1007/s40031-018-0323-y.

[19] S. Mirjalili, S.M. Mirjalili, A. Lewis, Grey wolf optimizer, Adv. Eng. Softw. 69 (2014) 46–61, https://doi.org/10.1016/j.advengsoft.2013.12.007.

[20] M. Panda, B. Das, Grey wolf optimizer and its applications: A survey, in: Lecture Notes in Electrical Engineering, Springer Verlag, 2019, pp. 179–194, https://doi.org/10.1007/978-981-13-7091-5_17.

[21] A.A.M. El-Gaafary, Y.S. Mohamed, A. Mohamed Hemeida, A.-A.A. Mohamed, Grey wolf optimization for multi input multi output system, Univ. J. Commun. Netw. vol. 3 (2015) 1–6, https://doi.org/10.13189/ujcn.2015.030101.

[22] Q. Al-Tashi, H. Md Rais, S.J. Abdulkadir, S. Mirjalili, H. Alhussian, A review of grey wolf optimizer-based feature selection methods for classification, in: Evolutionary Machine Learning Techniques, Springer, Singapore, 2020, pp. 273–286, https://doi.org/10.1007/978-981-32-9990-0_13.

Genetic algorithms: Principles and application in RAMS

Mohammad Ali Farsi

Reliability and standard group, A&S Research Institute, Ministry of Science, Research and Technology, Tehran, Iran

1. Introduction

Reliability engineers deal with several complicated problems during the design, manufacture, installation, and utilization of real-world systems; they need to overcome these and find an optimal solution. Different techniques such as genetic algorithm (GA), particle swarm (PS), simulated annealing (SA), and bat algorithm (BA) have been developed and applied to find the optimal solution or overcome engineering challenges and nondeterministic polynomial (NP) problems.

The GA was introduced by J. Holland based on the concept of Darwin's theory of evolution; it was initially used to simulate the biological evolution of adaptive natural systems. This algorithm is a significant field of artificial intelligence and operation research, which has been developed and modified to obtain the best solution for NP-hard problems. GA works based on a stochastic search in a complex landscape, and preserves the better species. In this algorithm, species compete for survival within the environment. Based on Darwin's theory, the weakest species are removed and those better adapted to the environment remain for the next step. The removed genotypes are replaced by the new species. This process is continued until all weak genotypes have been destroyed.

Based on these ideas, the following principles are applied in most of GAs to find the best solution [1]:

- The problem addressed defines the environment.
- Candidate solutions of the problem are presented by specified species or individuals, also known as *chromosomes.*
- Their *genotypes* encode the candidate solutions for the problem. The genotype phenotype translation establishes how the chromosomes should be interpreted to obtain the actual candidate solutions.
- The compatibility of chromosomes with the environment (predefined problem) determines the chromosome's chance for survival.
- There is an evolving population of chromosomes, where a new candidate may be produced and another removed.
- New candidates are generated based on *recombination and/or* mutation of others.

Nature-Inspired Computing Paradigms in Systems. https://doi.org/10.1016/B978-0-12-823749-6.00001-5

It should be noted that different algorithms have been proposed based on the mentioned principles since the 1960s. This chapter introduces general and practical guidelines to design and construct a GA for Reliability, Availability, Maintainability, and Safety (RAMS) problems optimization. Therefore, firstly, the GA construction, genetic operators, evolution model and replacement strategy, stop condition, and advantages and disadvantages of the GAs are presented. Then, GA applications in RAMS fields are investigated.

2. GA construction

For the optimization of a real-world problem, the problem should be carefully studied and all important parameters such as inputs and outputs must be defined. In GAs, each solution is presented as a chromosome, and each chromosome consists of several genes that introduce all of the significant parameters of the problem. This step, that a solution is presented or encoded as a chromosome, is a key issue in GA construction. All parameters should be mapped to chromosome factors from real space to modeled space, which is called the encoding process. The encoding methods can be grouped as follows [2]:

- Binary encoding;
- Real number encoding;
- Integer or literal permutation encoding; and
- General data structure encoding.

Although the binary method is the simplest technique used for encoding, this method may not be used for all types of problems. Real number encoding is the best approach for function optimization, and constrained optimization is used as the first option. *Integer or literal permutation encoding* is the best approach for combinatorial optimization problems because the essence of combinatorial optimization problems is the permutation or combinational items subjected to constraints. For more complicated problems, an appropriate data structure is proposed to define a gene to capture the nature of the problem.

The search process is started by an initial population generation. To generate these candidate solutions, different techniques may be used, such as random, diverse, and heuristic solutions. Algorithms proposed for the generation of the initial population commonly use the random strategy because it is the easiest, it has no bias, and initial data are not necessary. When a chromosome is randomly generated, sometimes this chromosome is located in an infeasible or illegal space. Usually, infeasible items can be controlled by a penalty approach and forced to select from the feasible regime. The algorithm should protect illegal items by reject or repair strategies.

The better chromosomes are selected by an evaluation process, because in Darwin's theory, stranger and better chromosomes have more chance for survival. Thus, the chromosomes compete and are evaluated by a fitness function. The fitness function is usually defined as an objective function. All solutions are evaluated and ranked to find the best or the weakest solution. After ranking, the new solutions should be generated for the next iteration. Roulette wheel selection, rank selection, Boltzmann selection, steady-state selection, tournament selection, and some others may be used to find the best chromosome [3].

2.1 **Genetic operators**

After the evaluation and definition of better solutions, a new population needs to be generated. The first population is defined as parent chromosomes, and a new population is generated by the combination of the parent chromosomes. The combination methodology is not clear, and an exact method has not been proposed for this task. Crossover and mutation operators are the GA components used to generate a new population (candidate solutions).

2.1.1 Crossover operator

The crossover operator is a general operator used to create a new solution. Through crossover, some parameters or genes are selected from parent A and others from parent B. The parents' selection is one of the main challenges in the GA for speedup to find the best practical solution. Different approaches have been proposed for selection of parents and genes. For instance, the best solution in the current step may be defined as A and other solutions may be defined as B. In another approach, A and B are randomly selected. After the parents' selection, the choosing of genes is very important. Which genes should be changed? And how many genes should be selected from A and B? Different combination of methods can be applied in this step. We do not have an exact or a clear idea for this operation [1]. In the following sections, two useful methods for crossover operators are presented.

(1) *Random selection*: In this approach, as the simplest way to create a new gene, this gene is randomly selected from A and B chromosomes. This procedure is repeated for the generation of all genes of a new chromosome (C). This approach is shown in Fig. 1.

(2) *Intelligent selection*: In this approach, to create a new gene, parents (A and B) are evaluated and the best genes from each are used to create a new gene. The best gene is selected based on a criterion (max., min., or average). This procedure is repeated for the generation of all genes of a new chromosome. This approach is shown in Fig. 2.

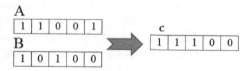

FIG. 1

Random crossover operator.

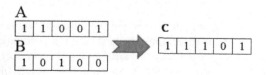

FIG. 2

Intelligent crossover operator (maximum value for offspring).

2.1.2 Mutation operation

Another operation to improve the search in solutions space is mutation. The mutation operation is strongly recommended to prevent falling in a local optimization point or limiting to one type of chromosome. The new offspring is randomly generated by the mutation operation. Random generation creates the opportunity to seek other points of the feasible space. This operation may be performed at a gene level or a chromosome level. The number of selected candidates and the selection procedure are very important. The candidates are usually selected from the weaker items or at random. The number of candidates mutated depends on the problem's complexity and the total number of chromosomes. Many works have suggested that the mutation operator should be performed on 5%–10% of the chromosomes [1, 4, 5]. Ordinarily, this number is determined by the trial and error method.

2.2 Adaptive and hybrid approaches in the GA

In engineering problems, we try to find the best solution in the shortest time and with reasonable accuracy. In some cases, the algorithm cannot find the global optimum and instead finds the local optimum point. This is in contrast to a global optimum, which is the optimal solution among all possible results, not just those in a particular neighborhood of values. In addition, in some cases we deal with an unefficient but time-consuming GA. Therefore, some research has been performed to improve the speed and accuracy of the search engine. Ordinarily, two strategies may be applied: adaptive or hybrid approaches.

In an adaptive strategy, the search process is changed during the optimization so that the procedure or its parameters are modified according to the algorithm feedback. For instance, in the initial steps, the number of candidates for the mutation operator is low and this number is slowly raised with iteration numbers; consequently, the chance is increased for the prevention of local optimization traps. In addition, in the crossover operation, the combination strategy may be changed by the procedure feedback. These schemes may be used for the local search around the optimal point. Recently, researchers have worked on a self-adaptive learning algorithm to increase the algorithm's efficiency. It should be noted that we can use different strategies together for this purpose.

Nowadays, different algorithms have been developed for the optimization process. Each algorithm has some advantages and disadvantages. Therefore, we can combine these algorithms to find a new algorithm that improves speed and accuracy. This new algorithm created by a combination process is called a hybrid algorithm. Different types of algorithms have been proposed for combination with the GA, such as particle swarm optimization (PSO), simulated annealing [6–9], the bat algorithm, and the ant colony algorithm. El-Mihoub et al. reviewed different methods of hybrid GAs [10]. The PSO algorithm is the most famous approach combined with the GA, and the new approach is called GA-PSO. In the next section, GA-PSO is briefly introduced.

2.2.1 The GA-PSO framework

The PSO algorithm is a powerful method to determine the optimum value of a complex function. It works based on particle movement and determines the best path via location/position and velocity control [6]. The PSO algorithm has memory. However, without a selection operator, PSOs may waste resources on poor individuals. If a GA and PSO are applied together, usually the time needed to find the optimal solution is decreased. Different approaches have been proposed and overlay the search process, which is divided into two sections: one section is performed by the GA and another by PSO. For example, the GA is used for global searches and PSO is used for local searches. Alternatively, in another approach, a portion of the population is created based on the GA, and at the same time, the remained portion is created by PSO [11].

3. Stop condition

GA uses an iteration procedure whereby in each iteration, two parents produce an offprint. In practical problems, we need criteria to interrupt this process and represent the final result. In this situation, it is said that the algorithm has converged and the evolution process is immediately stopped.

The following three kinds of termination conditions have been traditionally employed for GAs [12]:

- Define an upper limit for the number of iterations;
- Define a limit for the number of evaluations of the fitness function; or
- Define a specified value (excessively low) for significant changes between the generations.

The first two alternatives are used when the problem is simple or some knowledge about it is available to estimate the search procedure length. The third criterion, whose nature is adaptive, does not need such background or knowledge.

The first alternative is very simple and the algorithm is stopped when the number of generations reaches the specified limit/value. For instance, after 100 iterations, the algorithm represents the final results. This value for RAMS problems is commonly defined between 100 and 10,000 iterations.

In the second alternative, the convergence or divergence of a chromosome/gene to the defined limit is established by the GA designer through the definition of a preset percentage, which is a threshold that should be reached. For instance, when a given gene value for 95% of the population in a GA (binary encoding) reaches 1, it can be said that the gene has converged to the allele 1.

In the third iteration, the GA designer, according to the problem's complexity and application, defines a small value to evaluate the GA convergence. For instance, the designer decides to stop the optimization process where the difference between the best solutions or the average of two consecutive generations is less than 0.001.

4. GA applications

The GA as a powerful and strong tool to solve practical problems has been used in many works; annually, approximately 2500 scientific papers are published that use GAs [2]. Different types of GAs have been developed and applied in the reliability, risk, safety, and maintenance engineering fields. Overall, it can be said that where we deal with decision-making problems and determine the optimal solution, especially when problems have constraints or multicriteria should be considered, this algorithm is a good candidate to overcome the challenges. According to the literature, GAs are widely used to solve problems such as:

- Reliability-based design optimization;
- Reliability allocation problems;
- Redundancy allocation problems;

- Reliability test planning;
- Availability optimization of production sites;
- Inspection and maintenance planning;
- Spare parts inventory optimization; and
- Joint optimization of the above problems.

In the rest of the chapter, some works about GA applications are reviewed.

4.1 Reliability-based design optimization

Reliability is one of the most important criteria in the design phase of a system or component, especially if this system works in a critical industry or situations such as military, nuclear plant, chemical plant, or aerospace. Reliability may affect the design process and increase design duration and cost. Commonly, the value of the reliability is predefined as a requirement and a designer should change the design parameters to obtain a desired value for the reliability. For instance, in a composite structure, the designer uses first/second-order reliability to determine the reliability and can change materials, fiber direction, and the number of layers and dimensions to increase reliability; however, the cost and weight usually limit the designer. Therefore, The designer should balance these parameters to obtain the cheapest and lightest structure that confirms the reliability value. In the following section, a composite structure is considered to explain this idea.

Assume we have a semicylindrical shell (Fig. 3) that has a pressure load ($P = 250,000$ Pa) forced on it. This structure includes 28 layers of glass-epoxy, and the failure probability for this shell should be less than 0.0001. Mechanical and material parameters for this shell is described in Table 1.

Fiber direction is one of the main parameters that affects structural strength, and the designer can alter this to improve structural reliability. Fibers' direction can be set from 0 to 90 degrees (91 states)—in other words, each layer can be chosen from 91 cases. Thus, this structure can be produced in 91^{28} forms. The reliability of these forms is not the same. Different types of criteria are proposed to evaluate and model composite failures, such as Tsai-Hill, Tsai-Wu, and Hashin criteria [13].

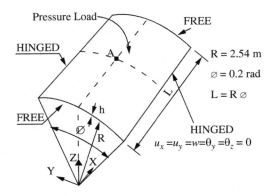

FIG. 3

Composite shell under pressure load [13].

Table 1 Mechanical properties and strengths for glass-epoxy.

E_1 (GPa)	E_2 (GPa)	v_{12}	v_{21}	G_{12} (GPa)	R_x (MPa)	R'_x (MPa)	R_y (MPa)	R'_y (MPa)	R_s (MPa)
55	18	0.25	0.08	8	1500	−1250	50	−200	100

The Hashin criteria (Eq. 1) is applied for this case study. A GA is driven with 20 chromosomes and stopped after 30 iterations. In this GA, 80% of the population are updated by crossover and 2% by mutation operators. A simple GA is used to find the optimum structure.

$$\left(\frac{\sigma_{11}}{X_T}\right)^2 + \frac{\sigma_{12}^2 + \sigma_{13}^2}{\sigma_{12}^2} = \begin{cases} \geq 1 \text{ fail} \\ < 1 \text{ safe} \end{cases}$$

$$\left(\frac{\sigma_{11}}{X_C}\right)^2 = \begin{cases} \geq 1 \text{ fail} \\ < 1 \text{ safe} \end{cases}$$

$$\frac{\sigma_{22}^2 + \sigma_{33}^2}{Y_T^2} + \frac{\sigma_{23}^2 + \sigma_{22}\sigma_{33}}{\sigma_{23}^2} + \frac{\sigma_{12}^2 + \sigma_{13}^2}{\sigma_{12}^2} = \begin{cases} \geq 1 \text{ fail} \\ > 1 \text{ safe} \end{cases} \tag{1}$$

$$\left[\left(\frac{Y_C}{2S_{23}}\right)^2 - 1\right]\left(\frac{\sigma_{22} + \sigma_{33}}{Y_C}\right) + \frac{\sigma_{22}^2 + \sigma_{33}^2}{4S_{23}^2} + \frac{\sigma_{23}^2 - \sigma_{22}\sigma_{33}}{S_{23}^2} + \frac{\sigma_{12}^2 + \sigma_{13}^2}{S_{12}^2}$$

$$= \begin{cases} \geq 1 \text{ fail} \\ > 1 \text{ safe} \end{cases}$$

Stresses and strains in the entire structure are calculated by Finite Element Method (FEM) packages such as ABAQUS and ANSYS (Fig. 4 shows composite layout in ABAQUS). These are used to evaluate the strength of the structure based on the Hashin criterion, and the reliability is then calculated by the first-order reliability method (FORM). The FORM is commonly used to estimate the reliability of structures and is based on random sampling from feasible space of parameters. In addition, it is an iterative solving procedure.

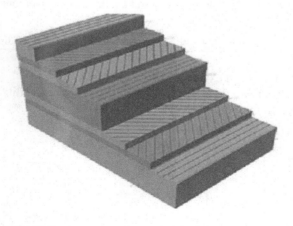

FIG. 4

Composite layers in the ABAQUS package.

In this problem, the main parameter is fiber direction that can be changed and should be determined. Each chromosome in the GA is defined by fiber directions of layers. A gene is an array with 28 items (chromosomes) that are randomly created. In each iteration, 20 samples are evaluated and the best chromosome with the maximum reliability value is detected. The GA is performed 30 times, and in each iteration we move closer to the best layout. When the procedure is stopped, the following structure is proposed to obtain the reliability equal to 99.99%: [90°, 89°, 90°, 46°, 45°, 45°, 90°] s [13].

4.2 Reliability allocation problems

Reliability allocation is an optimization process conducted to achieve a desired reliability value [14–16]. Commonly, the total cost should be minimized, and there are different types of constraints such as volume, mass, and technological limitations. In the allocation process, reliability characters of each component or subsystem are determined to achieve the desired goal. To explain this topic, consider a system that includes n components. The system reliability should be more than (R_G) and the cost function obtains its minimum value. This nonlinear problem is formulated as follows [14]:

$$P : \min C = \sum_{i=1}^{n} c_i(R_i)$$
$$\text{Constraints} : \begin{cases} R_S \geq R_G \\ R_{i,\min} \leq R_i \leq R_{i,\max} \end{cases} \tag{2}$$

where R_G is the predefined reliability of the system. C is the cost function calculated by an empirical relation as follows:

$$c_i\left(R_i, R_{i,\min}, R_{i,\max}\right) = e^{\left[(1-f_i)\cdots \frac{R_i - R_{i,\min}}{R_{i,\max} - R_i}\right]} \tag{3}$$

This is an exponential function and three parameters that play an important role in this relation are $R_{i,\min}$, $R_{i,\max}$, and f_i. However, $R_{i,\min}$ is the current (initial) value of the ith component reliability. The parameter $R_{i,\max}$ determines the maximum achievable reliability of the component. Finally, f_i is the feasibility function of the ith component, which depends on the complexity of the component, criticality, the state of the art, and the operational profile and availability of component I (α_i). This function may be defined as follows:

$$f_i = \alpha_i \times \frac{\text{complexity}(i) + \text{state}(i) + \text{operational profile}(i) + \text{criticality}(i)}{40} \tag{4}$$

Fig. 5 shows the cost function as an exponential function.

Consider the system shown in Fig. 6. The relation of the system reliability obtained using the decomposition method is given by:

$$R_S = (R_1 + R_2 - R_1 R_2)R_3 +$$
$$(1 - R_3) \left\{ \begin{array}{l} R_6 \left[\begin{array}{l} (R_4 + R_5 - R_4 R_5)(R_7 + R_8 - R_7 R_8)R_1 \\ + R_2 - (R_4 + R_5 - R_4 R_5)(R_7 + R_8 - R_7 R_8)R_1 R_2 \end{array} \right] + \\ (1 - R_6) \left[\begin{array}{l} (R_4 R_7 + R_5 R_8 - R_4 R_5 R_7 R_8)R_1 \\ + R_2 - (R_4 R_7 + R_5 R_8 - R_4 R_5 R_7 R_8)R_1 R_2 \end{array} \right] \end{array} \right\} \tag{5}$$

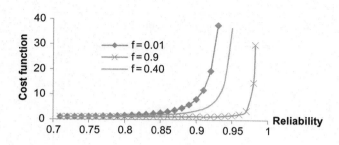

FIG. 5

The cost function.

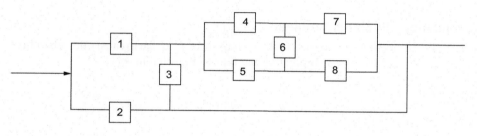

FIG. 6

System configuration for the reliability allocation problem.

A gene is defined by a vector with seven elements. Each element indicates a value for a component. These values are randomly selected according to the system constraints shown in Table 2. In this problem, 30 genes are used to create a GA. The reliability function is a nonlinear function and the reliability values are continuing; thus, we are dealing with an NP-hard problem. After 1000 iterations, the reliability values allocated to system components are determined as in Table 3.

Table 2 The inputs of the reliability allocation problem.

Component	$R_{i,\,min}$	$R_{i,\,max}$	f_i
1	0.7	0.999	0.3825
2	0.7	0.999	0.105
3	0.75	0.999	0.15
4	0.7	0.999	0.475
5	0.73	0.999	0.35
6	0.78	0.999	0.0975
7	0.75	0.999	0.435
8	0.71	0.999	0.465

Table 3 The optimal reliability allocated.	
Component	**Allocated reliability (R_i)**
1	0.956
2	0.953
3	0.973
4	0.943
5	0.73
6	0.953
7	0.923
8	0.913

4.3 Redundancy allocation problems

Generally, the reliability of the main parts of the system is not adequate to satisfy the reliability requirements. This can be improved by incorporating the following techniques [1]:

(1) Decreasing the complexity of the system;
(2) Using the better component that is more reliable; or
(3) Using structural redundancy.

Redundancy allocation as the main alternative has been selected in many works. The redundancy technique is a scheme whereby an original component is supported by other components. Different plans have been implemented, and the second component has been used in cold, warm, and hot situations [17, 18]. In cold redundancy, called cold standby, the alternative component is used when the first/original component has failed. In the hot situation, the alternative component works simultaneously with the original component and the forced loads are the same. In warm cases, the alternative component endures a portion of the loads that affect the original component.

Multilevel redundancy allocation (MLRA) is a redundancy allocation that may be considered at the system level (top level) or whole-of-system level. It should be noted that MLRA is a more complex problem. In the next sections, firstly traditional redundancy allocation for a complex system is explained, and then MLRA for a series system is discussed.

4.3.1 Redundancy allocation for a complex system

Assume a complex system with a bridge structure that includes five components (Fig. 7).
The reliability of the system is determined by the following equation:

$$R(s) = R_1R_2 + R_3R_4 + R_1R_4R_5 + R_2R_3R_5 - R_1R_2R_3R_4 - R_1R_2R_3R_5 - R_1R_2R_5R_4 - R_1R_5R_3R_4 - R_5R_2R_3R_4 \\ + 2R_1R_2R_3R_4R_5 \tag{6}$$

We wish to obtain the maximum value of the system reliability by determining the best number of redundancy for each component. This problem is subject to the following constraints [19, 20]:

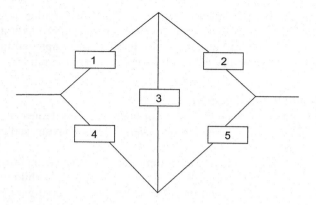

FIG. 7

The structure of a complex system.

$$\sum_{i=1}^{m} w_i v_i^2 n_i^2 \leq V,$$

$$\sum_{i=1}^{m} \alpha_i (-1000/\ln r_i)^{\beta_i} (n_i + \exp(n_i/4)) \leq C, \qquad (7)$$

$$\sum_{i=1}^{m} w_i n_i \exp(n_i/4) \leq W,$$

$$0 \leq r_i \leq 1, \; n_i \in \text{positive integer}, \; 1 \leq i \leq m.$$

where V is the upper limit on the sum of the subsystems' products of volume and weight, v_i is the volume of each component in subsystem i, W is the upper limit on the weight of the system, w_i is the weight of the ith component, r_i is the ith subsystem reliability, and C is the upper limit on the cost of the system. Table 4 shows the parameters used in this system modeling.

When the reliability of components is indicated as (0.814, 0.8646, 0.8903, 0.70119, and 0.73473), the final reliability for the system is 0.3587. This value is poor and we must utilize redundancy to improve the system performance. Hsieh et al. used a simple GA with 100 iterations to solve this problem [19]. Their GA used the following parameters: population size = 200; mutation rate = 0.85; and crossover rate = 0.03. The final configuration proposed for this system includes 13 components, as (3, 3, 3,

Table 4 The parameters used in the redundancy allocation of the complex system.

i	$10^5 \alpha_i$	$w_i v_i^2$	w_i	V	C	W
1	2.33	1	7	110	175	200
2	1.45	2	8			
3	0.541	3	8			
4	8.05	4	6			
5	1.95	2	9			

3, 1). The best reliability estimated is equal to 0.999879. This configuration creates a significant improvement in the system performance. This problem has been solved by a hybrid algorithm known as the GA-PSO (by Sheikhalishahi et al.) and the best reliability was improved to 0.999889 [20]. The GA-PSO improves the search capability to detect the optimum configuration.

4.3.2 Multilevel redundancy allocation

In this section, a multilevel serial system (Fig. 8) is considered. This is defined as a hierarchical system with the entire system at the topmost level, the subsystems at lower levels, and the components at the lowest level.

Redundancy could be configured to any unit from system level to component level. Once the redundancy is allocated to units at the parent level, there will be multiple child units at lower levels.

Thus, the reliability R_i of unit U_i for multilevel series and parallel configurations can be calculated using the following equations [21]:

$$R_i = \prod_{m}^{n_i} \left[1 - \prod_{j}^{x_i} \left(1 - R_{i,m}^j \right) \right] \tag{8}$$

$$R_i = 1 - \prod_{m}^{n_i} \left[\prod_{j}^{x_i} \left(1 - R_{i,m}^j \right) \right] \tag{9}$$

where $R_{i,m}^j$ are reliability values of the subunit $U_{i,m}^j$. Each $R_{i,m}^j$ value is calculated using the mentioned equation at the level immediately below the unit, and these computations are recursively iterated to the level just above the very lowest hierarchical level. Using Eqs. (8) and (9), the system reliability can be determined by:

$$R = 1 - \left(1 - \left[\left(1 - \prod_{j=1}^{3} \left(1 - R_{11}^j \right) \right) \left(R_{12}^1 \right) \right] \right)$$
$$\times \left(1 \left[\left(1 - \prod_{j=1}^{2} \left(R_{11}^j \right) \right) \left(1 - \prod_{j=1}^{2} \left(R_{12}^j \right) \right) \right] \right) \tag{10}$$

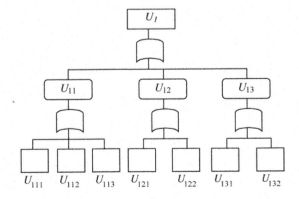

FIG. 8

A three-level series system.

Table 5 Input parameters of the MLRA problem.

Unit	Reliability	Cost	λ
U_{111}	0.9	5	3
U_{112}	0.95	6	4
U_{113}	0.85	5	4
U_{121}	0.85	7	4
U_{122}	0.90	6	4
U_{131}	0.9	8	3
U_{132}	0.8	7	4

Cost is commonly considered in redundancy allocation as a constraint. The cost of the mentioned system is calculated by Eq. (11):

$$C_{sys} = \left[\left(\sum_{j=1}^{3} C_{11}^{j} + (\lambda_{11})^3 \right) + (C_{12} + \lambda_{12}) \right]$$
$$+ \left[\left(\sum_{j=1}^{2} C_{11}^{j} + (\lambda_{11})^2 \right) + \left(\sum_{j=1}^{2} C_{12}^{j} + (\lambda_{12})^2 \right) \right] + (\lambda_1)^2 \tag{11}$$

where C_{ij} defines the cost of a unit and λ_{ij} is additional costs of the -[th] unit when adding a redundant unit to a unit. Assume that the system parameters are defined as in Table 5.

This problem is an NP-hard problem since it is very complex, and solutions space is complicated. Kumar et al. worked on this problem and developed a hierarchical GA to solve this challenge. They first used a traditional GA, and the obtained maximum reliability for the cost less than 290 is equal to 0.9276 [21]. When they used the hierarchical GA, the reliability was increased to 0.9742 [22]. This problem shows that traditional GA in some cases is weak and should be improved. In addition, adaptive or hybrid schemes are efficient for this purpose. For instance, Farsi used a GA-bat algorithm to solve this problem and achieve a value of 0.983 for the system reliability [23].

4.4 Inspection and maintenance planning for one-shot systems

The optimization process is not limited to the design stage of a product life cycle; we deal with complex situations for decision-making in all steps, such as process and product design, operations planning and control, and operations improvement. GAs have demonstrated considerable success in providing acceptable solutions in these fields. The operation and utilization phase is very important for commercial and industrial systems, and commonly about 10%–20% of operation cost is related to maintenance, since these systems are usually repairable or their performance is degraded during their lifetime. In other words, the uncorrected maintenance program can increase operation cost. Therefore, maintenance and inspection optimization can reduce operation costs; this ultimately helps to decrease production costs in manufacturing factories or reduce operation costs of companies such as airlines. Much research has been conducted to improve maintenance strategy selection or maintenance planning. In this section, to show the capability of GAs to solve maintenance problems, a one-shot system is considered and an optimal inspection plan is determined.

One-shot systems are reliable devices that operate at one time [24], and a user expects them to work successfully after a long storage life. Thus, they should be designed carefully and inspected while in storage, as they may be damaged or their performance can be reduced by degradation processes. In this section, an optimal inspection and test plan are proposed to ensure system reliability. Let us assume that a system consists of two types of components: components degrading over time and components that randomly fail. In this study, the reliability of the first type of components is modeled by a Weibull distribution, and the second type is modeled as exponential distribution. It is also assumed that the inspection and repair times may be ignored, and after repair, the reliability is increased but not as good as new. When the system reliability is reduced below a desired threshold, the whole of the system should be changed. According to the above assumptions, two types of parameters should be determined: inspection times and the number of tests in an inspection. The number of tests affects the reliability value —which should be demonstrated—and its confidence level. Increasing tests leads to increased cost.

The cost is a significant parameter in this problem and consists of three sections: the cost of the inspection and repair, the cost of the replaced components and the cost of components destroyed during destructive tests. The costs are defined as follows [25]:

$$C_1 = \sum_{i=1}^{N_1} C_{1i} + A$$

$$C_D = \sum_{i=1}^{N} \sum_{j=1}^{N_2} n_{ij} c_{Dj} \tag{12}$$

$$C_2 = \sum_{i=1}^{N_T} C_{2i}$$

where C_{1i} indicates the cost for ith inspection process, C_D defines the destructive test cost, and C_2 is the cost of replaced components. N_1 defines the number of components inspected by the nondestructive tests, N_2 indicates the number of components used in the destructive tests, N_T is the total number of the system components, and N introduces the number of inspections in a specified duration. According to system reliability, it is expected that most of the tests will be performed successfully. Thus, the reliability of zero failure components can be estimated [1, 25]:

$$E[\hat{r}] = \frac{n}{n+1} \tag{13}$$

$$\mathrm{var}(\hat{r}) = \frac{n}{(n+1)^2 (n+2)} \tag{14}$$

If the n value (the number of successful tests) is increased, the expected value is improved and variance is decreased, but the cost is increased. If a failure is recorded, then binomial distribution can be used to estimate the probability of success (reliability).

Assume a separation system of a sounding rocket[a] that includes different types of components (Fig. 9). According to expert opinion and history, we know that the system after 2089 days is expired, since its reliability is below a predefined threshold (0.8). Thus, we plan a program for inspection and component replacement to improve the system's lifetime.

---

[a]A sounding rocket is a scientific device that has been sent to space to study the atmosphere and other space-related topics.

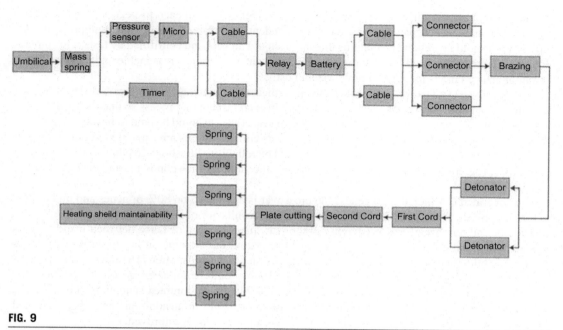

FIG. 9

The separation system configuration [26].

We know that the system reliability in storage time for gradational process and environment condition is reduced; on the other hand, in each inspection and replacement process, the system reliability is increased. We wish to find the optimal balance between these behaviors. The system configuration is series-parallel structure with more than 27 units. All of these can be inspected or tested, but the costs for inspection of some units such as timer, cable, and plates are very small and they are ignored in modeling. The inspection and replacement costs of the system components are shown in Table 6.

Table 6 Components cost in inspection and replacement process.

Component	Inspection cost	Replacement cost	Component	Inspection cost	Replacement cost
Umbilical	5	5000	Connector	1	100
Mass spring	5	500	Brazing	10	200
P.S.	–	2000	Detonator	–	50
Timer	–	200	Cords	–	100
Cable	–	10	Plates	–	50
Relay	1	1000	Spring	1	10
Battery	5	500	H.S.	15	100

The optimal inspection times (interval) and the number of tests in each inspection process are the goals of this study. These parameters are not independent; therefore, it is a complicated problem. We defines a threshold for reliability that this threshold should be kept and confirmed by tests. This threshold has been predefined as 0.8. We know that a maintenance program is reasonable and practical when the maintenance cost is less than a new system cost.

In this study, a GA is developed that each gene indicates a maintenance program consists of inspection duration and the number of tests are carried out in each inspection process so that the total inspections and replacements cost is less than a new system price (a cost should be paid to buy a new system). At the first step, according to the system cost, the inspection durations are estimated via random generation of the number of tests. These data are checked by reliability threshold. In other words, a feasible and correct program is created. These data in the GA procedure are then compared and the best solution is identified.

The generated GA includes 50 genes, and crossover is conducted on 80% of genes and mutation is performed on 5%. After 1000 iterations, the following results are obtained [25].

The optimal number of the inspection durations is three, and the distance between inspections is constant and equal to 1900 days. After the third inspection, the system can be stored for 1861 days and the reliability is reduced under the threshold level. In other words, after 7561 days, the inspection costs are greater than a new system price and the system should be replaced by a new system.

It should be noted that this problem is an NP-hard problem with complex state; thus, this work can be reconsidered and solved by hybrid algorithms to improve the result. In addition, the authors assumed that the inspection interval was constant, and this assumption can be improved.

4.5 Joint optimization of spare parts inventory and maintenance policies

Maintenance planning and spare parts inventory management are the main parts of system operation management. These can constitute a significant portion of the total production costs. Thus, modeling and evaluation-related costs are very important. These topics have been individually studied in many works [26–28]. Recently, with the development of the Industry 4.0 concept, modeling and optimization have been considered jointly, since the dependence between them cannot be ignored. Today, with the advance in monitoring and developing maintenance technologies and dependence increasing among systems, the spare parts management role is more important. Thus, some studies have been performed to achieve joint optimization of these processes. In this section, a manufacturing system is considered and the optimal plan for condition-based maintenance (CBM) and spare parts inventory is determined.

Assume that a machine has two critical units with a series structure that are monitored and maintained following a CBM policy. According to collected data and history, those reliabilities can be modeled based on a Weibull distribution. We know that component reliability is varied and degraded during working time; therefore, the spare part is commonly ordered before the stoppage since availability is decreased. Consequently, the spare parts must be ordered when the original part works and its reliability is above a predefined threshold. The spare parts may be ordered on time, but the machine may be stopped and the availability is decreased because of a delay in delivering. If spare parts are delivered sooner than the replacement time, they should be stored, and this means space and cost are required for storage. In this study, it is also assumed that spare parts are prepared by two suppliers. We wish to determine the best time for ordering, replacement, and also supplier selection to obtain the maximum availability with cost constraints. This problem is modeled as below:

Table 7 System parameters.

The first supplier factors for the first spare part: delivery time (100,22), cost = 4000, Weibull distribution (alpha = 5000, beta = 1.5)
The first supplier factors for the second spare part: delivery time (90,20), cost = 5500, Weibull distribution (alpha = 6000, beta = 1.4)
The second supplier factors for the first spare part: delivery time (70,5), cost = 8000, Weibull distribution (alpha = 7000, beta = 1.3)
The second supplier factors for the second spare part: delivery time (70,15), cost = 3500, Weibull distribution (alpha = 4000, beta = 1.3)
Storing: the cost for the standard condition storage is 30 per hour for the first spare part, and 20 for the second spare part.
CBM repair time for the first part follows a normal distribution as (40,3), and for the second part is (40,3).
CBM repair cost for the first part is 2000, and the second part is 1500.
The probability and chance to select the first supplier is between 0.2 and 0.8.
The ordering is conducted when the reliability is between 0.7 and 0.90.
The replacement is conducted when the reliability is between 0.8 and 0.95.

$$\text{Min. cost.}$$
$$\text{Availability} \geq A_0$$
$$S_{min} \leq S_i \leq S_{max}, \quad i = 1, 2, \ldots, 8$$

where S defines the critical parameters (e.g., chance for a supplier selection and reliability at ordering time and reliability at replacement time), and the min. and max. values of each parameter indicate thresholds for it. In this study, the system parameters are defined in Table 7.

The costs of the shutdown, maintenance, and spare parts inventory for this problem are derived by Eq. (15).

$$TC = \sum_{i=1}^{n} Cs_i + \sum_{i=1}^{n} CR_i + \sum_{h=1}^{l} Shc_h + \sum_{k=1}^{h} STC_k \tag{15}$$

where TC is the total cost, Cs_i defines the spare part cost, and CR_i indicates the replacement operation cost for a spare part. Stopping or shutdown events adds a system cost as ShC, and when a spare part should be stored, the STC_k indicates the cost for a spare part storing.

Note: Spare part cost and failure rate depend on supplier selection. In other words, the quality of components is not the same when they are prepared by different suppliers.

The total cost should be minimized, but the availability cannot be reduced from a predefined threshold ($A_0 = 0.85$). To find the optimal plan, a GA is developed. In the constructed GA, the crossover is performed on 80% of individuals, and mutation is conducted on 10% of them. Each program that is randomly created explains a gene. The availability of the system and total cost are determined by Monte Carlo simulation (an internal loop with 2000 iterations); these genes are then compared to detect the best gene. For the crossover process, in this case, the average behavior of genes is considered. The best gene is kept, but the crossover procedure is conducted on selected genes using the average of properties. The framework developed for this problem is presented in Fig. 10 [29].

The stop condition is defined as the difference between the two generations. This should be less than 0.1. After 100 iterations, the following data (Table 8) are proposed to obtain a reasonable system.

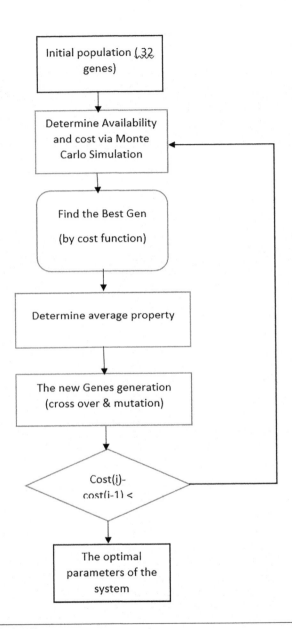

FIG. 10

The framework of the optimization process.

Table 8 The best values of the system parameters.

Cost	Availability	First ordering time	First repair time	First supp. Prob.	First storing cond.	Second ordering time	Second repair time	First supp. Prob.[a]	Second storing cond.
9522	0.870	0.8553	0.86	0.595	1	0.8578	0.8796	0.4203	3

Note: The authors in system modeling used the maintenance opportunity scheme, since this scheme merges two or more tasks close together, and it can reduce total cost and increase system availability [30]. This factor has been selected as 12%—in other words, the time of each task may be varied (conducted sooner or later) for a combination of two tasks [29].
[a] The first supplier probability to select as the provider of the second spare part.

5. Industry 4.0 and optimization

In the last decade, the integration of the digital, physical, and human worlds has increased significantly and we are witnessing the fourth industrial revolution, known as Industry 4.0. Factories are designed as open platforms and distributed systems with a dynamic structure. We believe that they are more efficient, faster, flexible, and resilient, with complex supply chains. Today, we deal with a smart system that is a system of systems with a dynamic structure. This change in industry improves the manufacturing and business environment and increases system speed, dependency, and complexity.

The Industry 4.0 paradigm will be implemented in all future factories. This concept was introduced based on smart manufacturing systems, but the idea can be applied in different industries, such as chemical plants, nuclear plants, and power plants. Industry 4.0 has several benefits: it reduces human interfaces, increases production speed and quality, ensures fast responses to customer requirements, and reduces production waste. However, we are dealing with challenges such as system modeling and Big Data. In addition, in this concept, new and unknown failure mechanisms, and unfamiliar dependencies among system components are appeared. Therefore, reliability engineers are dealing with new and unknown hazards and risks that should be considered in the analysis. Risk and reliability considerations for these types of systems are necessary. In other words, reliability optimization is at the heart of reliability engineering. Therefore, the determination of the optimal situation for real systems should be noted when Industry 4.0 is implemented.

The optimization process in the Industry 4.0 context is crucial because it deals with dynamic and resilient structures to generate different types and a huge volume of data. These data should be analyzed online since the system provides a real-time response. Moreover, several disciplines, software, and hardware are integrated in an Industry 4.0 context; thus, in reliability optimization of modern complex systems, the following challenges should be considered [31]:

(i) New and updated information generation because of integration and response to continuous streams of data;

(ii) There are all sorts of uncertainties that affect the decision-making framework and system reliability optimization;

(iii) The integration of different disciplines in Industry 4.0. Each discipline cooperates with individual objectives that should be optimized within an overall system optimization;

(iv) The simultaneous optimization of reliability in design, manufacturing, and operation steps. Spare parts inventory and logistics management influence should also be considered; and

(v) Dynamic optimization because of the variation of conditions for evolving systems.

In a nutshell, online optimization with high-speed computation is necessary. Different algorithms may present themselves as candidates, but the time-consuming reduction is a significant factor in the selection process. Although GAs——either traditional or hybrid algorithms—are one of the first candidates for optimizaion problems, they should be improved to increase accuracy and reduce time-consuming processes. Therefore, studies on these algorithms should continue.

6. Advantages and disadvantages of the GA

A GA is an evolutionary algorithm optimizer that is a global optimization method. It can easily be understood and adjusted to the problem at hand. All parameters and any aspect of the algorithm may be customized and modified. GAs always generate an answer, and the answer gets better with time. GAs can work in a noisy environment and support multiobjective problems. The search process starts from individual points that help us to search in a large and wide solution space. The capability to combine GAs with other algorithms is a notable parameter that increases algorithm performance. GAs can be parallelized to increase algorithm capability and speed [32]. Recent research has been conducted to increase GA efficiency by hybrid and adaptive algorithms [33] because speed and accuracy in Big Data situations and online systems need to be improved.

On the other hand, although GAs are applied in different fields of reliability and maintenance engineering, the results obtained in some cases are poor and other algorithms may work better. The GA principle is easy, but its implementation is still an art. GAs needs less information about the problem; however, objective function, encoding, and operators rights may be complicated. Finally, the GA is an expensive computational algorithm, especially in terms of time; therefore, its design, construction, and implementation should be conducted carefully.

7. Conclusion

In this chapter, the GA as a powerful tool for optimization applied frequently in scientific or industrial problems has been considered. An ordinary GA creates a solution for different types of problems, either constrained or unconstrained, and this has improved with time. Reliability optimization is at the heart of reliability engineering and provides better utilization of the system. The GA is an easy algorithm used for modeling and optimization of different aspects of RAMS problems. Some applications of the GA have been presented in this chapter; usually, GA is selected as the first option for the optimization of different types of engineering problems. Although the GA is powerful, for complicated problems, the convergence speed needs to be increased. Therefore, hybrid and adaptive algorithms are recommended for these types of problems. Recently, parallel GAs have been developed and used for reliability optimization. In addition, the Industry 4.0 concept creates new challenges and GAs need to be upgraded to overcome these.

References

[1] M.A. Farsi, Principles of Reliability Engineering, Simayeh Danesh, Tehran, 2016.
[2] Carlos García-Martínez, Francisco J. Rodriguez, and Manuel Lozano, Genetic Algorithms, Chapter of Handbook of Heuristics, Springer, https://doi.org/10.1007/978-3-319-07124-4_28, 201.

[3] M. Mitchell, An Introduction to Genetic Algorithms, The MIT Press, 1996. ISBN: 9780262133166.

[4] M. Agarwal, R. Gupta, Genetic search for redundancy optimization in complex systems, J. Qual. Maint. Eng. 12 (4) (2006) 338–353.

[5] R. Tavakkoli-Moghaddam, J. Safari, F. Sassani, Reliability optimization of series-parallel systems with a choice of redundancy strategies using a genetic algorithm, Reliab. Eng. Syst. Saf. 93 (2008) 550–556.

[6] R. Abbasnia, M. Shayanfar, A. Khodam, Reliability-based design optimization of structural systems using a hybrid genetic algorithm, Struct. Eng. Mech. 52 (6) (2014) 1099–1120, https://doi.org/10.12989/SEM.2014.52.6.1099.

[7] M. Mukuda, Y.S. Yun, M. Gen, Reliability optimization problems using adaptive hybrid genetic algorithms, J. Adv. Comput. Intell. Intell. Inf. 8 (4) (2004) 1–5.

[8] A. Gaun, G. Rechberger, H. Renner, Probabilistic reliability optimization using hybrid genetic algorithms, in: Proceedings of the 2010 Electric Power Quality and Supply Reliability Conference, 2010, pp. 151–158. Kuressaare https://doi.org/10.1109/PQ.2010.5550003.

[9] B. Dalanezi Mori, H. Fiori de Castro, K. Lucchesi Cavalca, Development of hybrid algorithm based on simulated annealing and genetic algorithm to reliability redundancy optimization, Int. J. Qual. Reliab. Manag. 24 (9) (2007) 972–987. https://doi.org/10.1108/02656710710826225.

[10] T.A. El-Mihoub, A. Adrian, L.N. Hopgood, A. Battersby, Hybrid Genetic algorithms: a review, Eng. Lett. 3 (2) (2006).

[11] A.M. Manasrah, H.B. Ali, Workflow scheduling using hybrid GA-PSO algorithm in cloud computing, Wirel. Commun. Mob. Comput. (2018), https://doi.org/10.1155/2018/1934784, 1934784.

[12] M. Safe, J. Carballido, I. Ponzoni, N. Brignole, On stopping criteria for genetic algorithms, in: Proceeding of Advances in Artificial Intelligence - SBIA 2004 conference, Brazil, 2004, pp. 405–413.

[13] N. Khobchehreh, M.A. Farsi, J. Fazilaity, Reliability Analysis of Laminated Composite Structures Using Finite Elements and Fist Order Reliability Method, MSc Thesis, Aerospace Research Institute, 2018.

[14] M.A. Farsi, B.I. Jahromi, Reliability allocation of a complex system by genetic algorithm method, in: Proceeding of International Conference on Quality, Reliability, Risk, Maintenance, and Safety Engineering—ICQR2MSE, China, Chengdu, 2011, pp. 1046–1049.

[15] D.W. Coit, E. Zio, The evolution of system reliability optimization, Reliab. Eng. Syst. Saf. 192 (2019) 106259–106302.

[16] O.S. Vaidya, L. Ganapathy, S. Kumar, A cost minimization model for system reliability allocation, Int. J. Qual. Reliab. Manag. 36 (9) (2019) 1620–1643, https://doi.org/10.1108/IJQRM-07-2018-0199.

[17] M. Modarres, M. Kaminskiy, V. Krivtsov, Reliability Engineering and Risk Analysis: A Practical Guide, CRC Press, 2009.

[18] X.-Y. Li, Y.-F. Li, H.-Z. Huang, Redundancy allocation problem of phased-mission system with non-exponential components and mixed redundancy strategy, Reliab. Eng. Syst. Saf. 199 (July 2020), https://doi.org/10.1016/j.ress.2020.106903.

[19] Y.-C. Hsieh, T.-C. Chen, D.L. Bricker, Genetic algorithms for reliability design problems, Microelectron. Reliab. 38 (1998) 599–1605.

[20] M. Sheikhalishahi, V. Ebrahimipour, H. Shiri, H. Zaman, M. Jeihoonian, A hybrid GA–PSO approach for reliability optimization in redundancy allocation problem, Int. J. Adv. Manuf. Technol. 68 (2013) 317–338.

[21] R. Kumar, K. Izui, M. Yoshimura, S. Nishiwaki, Multilevel redundancy allocation optimization using hierarchical genetic algorithm, IEEE Trans. Reliab. 57 (4) (2008) 650–661.

[22] R. Kumar, K. Izui, Y. Masataka, Optimal multilevel redundancy allocation in series and series–parallel systems, Comput. Ind. Eng. 57 (2009) 169–180.

[23] M.A. Farsi, Development a new algorithm for optimal multi-level redundancy allocation, in: Proceeding of ESREL, Poland, 2014.

[24] Y. Cheng, E.A. Elsayed, Reliability modeling and optimization of operational use of one-shot units, Reliab. Eng. Syst. Saf. 176 (2018) 27–36, https://doi.org/10.1016/j.ress.2018.03.021.

[25] A. Mehrvarz, M.A. Saniei Monfared, M.A. Farsi, M. Shafiee, Condition monitoring and reliability maintenance optimization of one-shot systems, Sharif J. Ind. Eng. Manag. 34.1 (1.1) (2018) 73–85.

[26] M.A. Farsi, A. Eslami, R. Gorgin, Reliability assessment of separation system via FMEA and RBD, J. Space Sci. 2 (2014) 30–36.

[27] X. Chen, D. Xu, L. Xiao, Joint optimization of replacement and spare ordering for critical rotary component based on condition signal to date, Eksploatacja I Niezawodnosc—Maint. Reliab. 19 (1) (2017) 76–85, https://doi.org/10.17531/ein.2017.1.11.

[28] A. Van Horenbeek, J. Buré, D. Cattrysse, L. Pintelon, P. Vansteenwegen, Joint maintenance and inventory optimization systems: a review, Int. J. Prod. Econ. 143 (2) (2013) 499–508, https://doi.org/10.1016/j.ijpe.2012.04.001.

[29] M.A. Farsi, E. Zio, Modeling and analyzing supporting systems for smart manufacturing systems with stochastic, technical and economic dependences, J. Adv. Des. Manuf. Technol. **13** (**4**) (2020).

[30] X. Zhang, J. Zeng, Joint optimization of condition-based opportunistic maintenance and spare parts provisioning policy in multiunit systems, Eur. J. Oper. Res. 262 (2) (2017) 479–498, https://doi.org/10.1016/j.ejor.2017.03.019.

[31] M.A. Farsi, E. Zio, Industry 4.0: some challenges and opportunities for reliability engineering, Int. J. Reliab. Risk Saf. Theory Appl. 2 (1) (2019) 23–34, https://doi.org/10.30699/ijrrs.2.1.4.

[32] H. Kim, P. Kim, Reliability-redundancy allocation problem considering optimal redundancy strategy using parallel genetic algorithm, Reliab. Eng. Syst. Saf. 159 (2017) 153–160.

[33] N. Demo, M. Tezzele, G. Rozza, A Supervised Learning Approach Involving Active Subspaces for an Efficient Genetic Algorithm in High-Dimensional Optimization Problems, Published on-Line, Research Gate, Jun 2020.

Evolutionary optimization for resilience-based planning for power distribution networks

Nariman L. Dehghani, Chi Zhang, and Abdollah Shafieezadeh
Risk Assessment and Management of Structural and Infrastructure Systems (RAMSIS lab), The Ohio State University, Columbus, OH, United States

1. Introduction

Power outages pose significant economic and social impacts on communities around the world. The increasing reliance of the society on electricity reduces the tolerance for power outages, and consequently highlights the need for enhancing the power grid resilience against natural hazards. Although these hazards are low-probability events, even one occurrence of an extreme event can be catastrophic for infrastructure systems. For instance, in 2017, Hurricane Harvey reached Texas as a Category 4 hurricane and resulted in severe damage to the built infrastructure [1, 2]. While the likelihoods of occurrence are small relative to other disturbances, they are not significantly small. For example, over the past four decades, the state of Texas has experienced weather-related events with a frequency of 1.7 events per year [2]. Thus, it is necessary to prepare infrastructure systems against these low-probability high-consequence events in hazard prone regions by adopting some strategies [3]. Recent extreme weather-related events induced substantial damage in electric infrastructure and left large numbers of customers without power [4]. In fact, extreme climatic events, such as hurricanes, have caused over 80% of the power outages in the United States [5]. As a recent example, on October 2020, Hurricane Zeta hit the Gulf of Mexico and left over 2.6 million residents without power, while it only reached a Category 2 hurricane at its peak [6]. Among the components of the power grid, power distribution networks (PDNs) are the most vulnerable in the face of extreme climatic events [7,8]. Thus, given the devastating regional and national consequences that hurricanes can incur and the ever-increasing reliance of the society on electricity, hurricane resilience enhancement of PDNs is crucial for public safety and economic prosperity.

Resilience is the ability of a system to absorb shocks and to quickly recover from disturbances [9–11]. Resilience is deemed as a comprehensive risk-based measure due to its ability to reflect on both the damage that the system has sustained, which is the concern of reliability, and the recovery performance of the system. Several studies have attempted to improve resilience of PDNs via planning (e.g., [12,13]). An effective strategy for resilience enhancement of PDNs is replacement of deteriorated utility poles with new ones, however, this action is costly. Unlike the corrective maintenance strategy that is applied after the occurrence of a failure, preventive maintenance is performed prior to a potential failure to decrease the likelihood of disruption in the services provided by the system. The latter maintenance contains a wide range of practices, from periodic chemical treatment to replacing poles with new wood poles or even new poles with durable construction materials (e.g., [14,15]). In practice, utility companies perform annual inspection and preventive maintenance actions to ensure the safety of PDNs. In fact, the National Electric Safety Code (NESC) [16] mandates utilities to replace deteriorated wood poles with new ones. The NESC prioritizes replacement of wood utility poles based on the remaining strength of these structures. This strategy is followed in over 90% of US states as a hardening solution to increase the hazard reliability of PDNs [17]. More specifically, the NESC requirement mandates replacing poles, once their remaining strength falls below two-thirds of the initial strength. This preventive maintenance strategy is not adequate, as it does not consider all the factors that affect the failure probability of poles. Reliability-based management can be a remedy to address this limitation of NESC strategy. Although reliability-based management considers the failure probability of poles in finding optimal preventive maintenance actions, it does not take into account the importance of poles for network services in the decision-making process. Similar to reliability-based management, the NESC strength-based strategy also does not consider the risks associated with the failure of poles. For example, a utility pole that serves a few customers can have a higher failure probability than a pole that serves a large number of customers. If the consequences of failure for network services are not considered in the decision-making, replacing the former pole becomes the priority because it plays a more important role in the reliability of the system. However, if the network consequences of failure are considered via a risk-based framework, replacing the latter pole could be more beneficial to the PDN, as it can reduce the number of power outages in the case that a hurricane hits the system. Risk-based management of systems has been investigated for different structures exposed to extreme events, such as bridges [18–20], buildings [21–23], and levee infrastructure systems [24]. In the case of utility poles, risk-based prioritization strategies (e.g., [25,26]) have been proposed as an alternative to the NESC strength–based strategy. For example, the authors proposed a risk metric called expected outage reduction (EOR) to prioritize pole replacements based on the expected power outage reduction if an existing pole is replaced by a new pole [25]. Nevertheless, the lack of integration with optimization techniques questions the optimality of these preventive maintenance strategies.

Given the limited available budget and resources, optimization is required to facilitate optimal preventive maintenance of large systems. Motivated by this fact, the authors developed a mixed-integer nonlinear programming (MINLP) model and solved this model by branch and bound (BB) algorithm to determine the optimal preventive maintenance planning for resilience enhancement of PDNs [27]. In this chapter, the authors investigate the application of an evolutionary algorithm (EA) to determine optimal preventive maintenance actions for life-cycle resilience enhancement of PDNs. More specifically, this chapter presents a decision-making framework for resilience enhancement of PDNs that are susceptible to gradual deterioration and face the risk of exposure to multiple stochastic hurricane events during the decision horizon. The proposed framework integrates modeling of hurricane hazards, performance of physical components of PDNs, and probabilistic resilience quantification to form a nonlinear constrained optimization problem (CoP) with binary decision variables. This optimization model facilitates the risk-based management of PDNs, with the objective of maximizing the life-cycle resilience by determining optimal preventive maintenance actions. The major complexity of this optimization problem arises from the large number of combinations of possible maintenance actions over an extended decision horizon as well as the existing constraints.

Given the complexity and scale of the CoP for resilience enhancement, an EA is presented herein to solve the problem. EAs are a subset of metaheuristic algorithms, which combine the randomization and local search inspired by natural phenomena to solve global optimization problems. Inspired by the biological evolution, EAs have become a type of simple and effective optimization tool without requiring much specific domain knowledge. EAs usually start with a randomly generated population that is evolved over subsequent generations. One key feature of EAs is that the best individuals are combined to form the next generation, allowing the population to be optimized over generations.

EAs include several primary groups of techniques such as genetic algorithm (GA) [28], genetic programming (GP) [29], evolution strategy (ES) [30], and differential evolution (DE) [31]. As an important branch of EAs, DE was originally introduced by Storn and Price [31]. Similar to other EAs, DE is a population-based optimization algorithm that solves difficult optimization problems. The straightforward implementation procedure of DE has increased its application in many fields. DE has three main advantages: (1) it is able to find the true global minimum of a multimodal search space regardless of the initial parameter values, (2) it has fast convergence, and (3) it requires limited control parameters [32]. DE was originally designed for solving unconstrained optimization problems. However, thanks to the popularity and potential of DE, techniques based on DE have been developed for solving CoPs [33–36]. DE has also been applied to problems concerning binary variables [37–45], which fit the profile of the problem discussed herein.

This chapter presents a binary differential evolution (BDE) algorithm for constrained optimization problems and applies the method for optimal resilience enhancement of PDNs. This algorithm, called BICDE, is the integration of the BDE algorithm proposed by Gong and Tuson [38] with the improved $(\mu+\lambda)$-constrained differential evolution (ICDE) algorithm proposed by Jia et al. [36]. The rest of this chapter is outlined as follows: in Section 2, an overview of the studied PDN is presented and the details of the optimization model are provided. A more detailed introduction of DE, BDE, the constraint-handling strategy, and the IBCDE algorithm is provided in Section 3 of this chapter. Section 4 discusses the results of this study. Finally, in Section 5, conclusions of this chapter are presented.

2. Problem description and formulation

To maximize the hurricane resilience of a PDN over an extended planning horizon via preventive maintenance, it is necessary to solve an optimization problem. In this section, first, the studied PDN is described. Then, the details of the preventive maintenance actions are presented. After that, the elements of the optimization model, including the objective function and constraints, are introduced. It is worth noting that the proposed resilience maximization model for PDNs is general and can be applied to different hazards with minor adjustments. If the studied hazard varies, the hazard model in the probabilistic resilience quantification process, which is described in Section 2.3, will be changed.

2.1 Power distribution network

The studied PDN is assumed to be in Harris County, Texas, United States. The system contains 7051 wood utility poles, 115 protective devices, and three substations. More details about this PDN can be found in the previous works by the authors (e.g., [8,25,27]). In this network, nodes represent utility poles that are vulnerable to hurricanes. It is assumed that power outages occur only due to the failure of the poles. If a node fails, protective devices cut off the power to downstream branches to prevent damage. Thus, the number of power outages is estimated as the number of nodes that are disconnected to any substation after a hurricane.

2.2 Preventive maintenance actions

There are two main categories of maintenance: (1) corrective maintenance that is applied if a failure is observed in the system and (2) preventive maintenance which is performed before observing any failure in the system. The main purpose of preventive maintenance actions is to reduce failures in the future. This study determines the optimal preventive actions for the described PDN over the life cycle of 100 years (i.e., $T_{LC} = 100$). In practice, long-term plans are divided into short-term planning periods (also known as operation plans) [8,46]. These short-term planning periods for PDNs are often three years [8,46]. Accordingly, the maintenance decisions here are made every three years (i.e., $\delta = 3$). Therefore, the life cycle of the PDN is discretized into 33 short-term decision periods (i.e., $N_T = 33$). At each decision period, there are two possible actions per pole, including either replacing the pole with a new pole with the same class and height or doing nothing. Due to the large number of poles in the network, at each time step, there are 7051 maintenance variables. To overcome the curse of dimensionality, herein, poles are categorized into 15 clusters (i.e., $N_C = 15$) with almost equal sizes (~6.7% of the poles in the system per cluster) and poles in each cluster receive the same action. Therefore, the maintenance variable for each cluster l at each period k becomes a binary variable $x_{l,k} \in \{0, 1\}$, where 1 and 0 indicate replacing the poles in that cluster and doing nothing, respectively. Considering that $N_T = 33$ and $N_C = 15$, there are 495 variables (i.e., 33×15) in this optimization problem. It is worth noting that the proposed optimization model is concerned with long-term planning.

2.3 Objective function

Before presenting the details of objective function, it is necessary to briefly explain the process of probabilistic resilience quantification. To quantify the probabilistic resilience of the PDN against hurricane events, four components are needed, including (1) probabilistic hurricane hazard model, (2) probability of failure of wood utility poles, (3) system performance model, and (4) system recovery model. These components are described as follows.

The hazard model probabilistically describes hurricane characteristics that are important for the PDN performance. Herein, wind speed as the hazard intensity and wind direction are considered as significant features of the hurricanes. According to [25], the probability density function of wind speed in Harris County follows a Weibull distribution with scale parameter of 45.4 and shape parameter of 1.2. Moreover, the probability density function of wind direction is uniformly distributed between 0 and 180 degrees [25].

PDNs consist of a large number of poles; a set of structural components that vary in their features. For instance, the span length, class, age, and height of poles as well as the number and diameter of conductors may vary from one pole to another pole. Probabilistic risk and resilience analyses of PDNs require estimation of the failure probability of poles for different scenarios of the hurricanes. Fragility models facilitate estimation of failure probabilities for these many scenarios. More details about fragility models of wood utility poles can be found in the previous works of the authors in [47–49]. This study uses a set of multidimensional wind fragility models of wood utility poles, which is introduced in

[49]. Features of a pole, wind speed, and wind direction are inputs to these models, and the pole's failure probability is the output of the models. Fragility models offer the failure probability of poles conditional on hazard intensities if key features of utility poles are fully known. However, this is not the case for long-term resilience quantification because the age of poles is uncertain due to possible prior failures and the subsequent corrective maintenance actions. In other words, preventive maintenance actions are applied to reduce the chance of future failures. However, even with frequent and widespread preventive maintenance actions, a percentage of poles in the PDN may fail under a future hurricane. In these conditions, utility companies perform corrective maintenance and replace the failed poles with new poles. As the age of poles has a significant impact on their failure probability, it is crucial to consider the impact of corrective maintenance on the age, and consequently on the failure probability of poles. To address this issue, a recursive formulation was introduced by the authors in [8,25] for pole vulnerability analysis. The formulation considers the probability of all possible corrective maintenance actions as well as the planned preventive maintenance actions during the entire planning horizon. Using this formulation, the time-dependent failure probability of poles can be estimated.

After estimating the failure probability of all utility poles in the network, the performance of the PDN after a hurricane event can be defined in terms of the number of customers without power. Then, a recovery model is applied to replace the failed utility poles. In this study, the time to replace a failed pole and the repair time of a conductor are each considered to follow a normal distribution with a mean of 5 h and a standard deviation of 2.5 h, and a mean of 4 h and a standard deviation of 2 h, respectively. For a specific hurricane event, the abovementioned process should be followed, and consequently the quality (Q) of the power can be estimated as a function of time as follows:

$$Q(t) = 100 \left(1 - \frac{N_o(t)}{N_t} \right) \tag{1}$$

where $N_o(t)$ is the number of customers without power at time t and N_t is the total number of customers in the PDN. This procedure should be repeated for a large number of realizations to consider the uncertainty in the quality of the PDN. Then, the expected resilience of the PDN can be computed as follows:

$$R = \frac{\int_0^{t_c} E[Q(t)]\, dt}{t_c} \tag{2}$$

where t_c is the control time assumed as 30 days. More details about probabilistic hurricane resilience quantification of PDNs can be found in the previous works by the authors (e.g., [8,25,27]).

As the objective is to maximize the life-cycle hurricane resilience of the PDN, the objective function is defined here as a function of the expected resilience of the PDN as:

$$\sum_{k=1}^{N_T} \log_{10} \left(1 - \frac{R_k}{100} \right) \tag{3}$$

where R_k denotes the expected resilience of the PDN at the decision period k. Evaluating the objective function in Eq. (3) is time-consuming. To improve the computational time of the optimization problem, instead of direct calculation of the expected resilience at each decision period (i.e., R_k), a multilayer perceptron neural network is developed to estimate the R_k in Eq. (2). This model consists of six hidden layers with 128, 64, 32, 16, 8, and 4 hidden units, respectively. ReLU activation is adopted for all the hidden layers and the Adam optimization algorithm is applied to minimize the loss function.

2.4 Constraints

Three constraints are defined in this optimization model, including for (1) the total number of pole replacements, (2) the number of pole replacements per period, and (3) the time between two subsequent pole replacements.

2.4.1 Total number of replacements

In this study, the performance of the optimal preventive maintenance strategy, which is obtained by the optimization model, is compared to the pole replacement strategy set by NESC. Thus, to make a fair comparison between these two preventive maintenance strategies, the total number of replacements is limited to 14,102 poles for the entire planning horizon (i.e., 100 years). This limit is equivalent to replacing all the clusters in the PDN two times. This constraint is selected because following the NESC approach, 14,102 poles are replaced over the planning horizon. This constraint is defined as follows:

$$\sum_{k=1}^{N_T} \sum_{l=1}^{N_C} x_{l,k} \leq TL \tag{4}$$

where TL stands for the limit on the total number of cluster replacements. TL is set to 30, which indicates 14,102 pole replacements.

2.4.2 Replacements per period

The number of pole replacements cannot surpass a limit per period of decision-making because of the limited budget and other required resources that are available to utilities. As discussed in [8,27], the maximum number of replacements per period (i.e., three years) is set to two clusters per period (i.e., ~13.3% of the poles in the PDN). This constraint is defined as follows:

$$\sum_{l=1}^{N_C} x_{l,k} \leq PL, \quad ke = 1,...,N_T \tag{5}$$

where PL is the limit on the number of cluster replacements per period, which is set to 2.

2.4.3 Subsequent replacements

As shown by the authors in [49], the failure probability of a new wood utility pole does not change significantly within the first 25 years. Thus, to avoid replacing a new pole within 8 decision periods (i.e., 24 years), a constraint is defined as follows:

$$\sum_{l=1}^{N_C} y_l \leq 0, \quad y_l = \begin{cases} 1, & \text{if cluster } l \text{ is replaced twice within 8 periods} \\ 0, & \text{Otherwise} \end{cases} \tag{6}$$

where y_l is a binary variable that indicates whether cluster l is replaced two times in less than 8 decision periods.

2.5 Model

In compliance with the above objective function and constraints, the optimization problem is modeled as follows:

$$\min_{x} \sum_{k=1}^{N_T} \log_{10}\left(1 - \frac{R_k}{100}\right)$$

$$\text{s.t.} \quad x_{l,k} = 0 \text{ or } 1, \qquad l = 1,\ldots,N_C; \quad k = 1,\ldots,N_T$$

$$\sum_{k=1}^{N_T}\sum_{l=1}^{N_C} x_{l,k} \leq TL$$

$$\sum_{l=1}^{N_C} x_{l,k} \leq PL, \qquad k = 1,\ldots,N_T \tag{7}$$

$$\sum_{l=1}^{N_C} y_l \leq 0, \quad y_l = \begin{cases} 1, & \text{if cluster } l \text{ is replaced twice within 8 periods} \\ 0, & \text{Otherwise} \end{cases}$$

Minimizing the objective function in this optimization model yields the optimal preventive maintenance strategy for maximizing the resilience of the PDN.

3. Solution methodology

The major complexity of solving this optimization model arises from the large number of decision variables as well as the existing constraints. To overcome these challenges, this study presents the BICDE algorithm, which is an integration of the binary differential evolutionary (BDE) algorithm proposed by Gong and Tuson [38] and the improved $(\mu+\lambda)$-constrained differential evolution (ICDE) proposed by Jia et al. [36]. The BICDE has the capability of the ICDE to solve constrained optimization problems and features of the BDE algorithm to handle nonlinear, nondifferentiable, and multimodal objective functions with binary decision variables. More specifically, in BICDE, the mutation and crossover are based on the BDE algorithm, while the selection is handled via an archiving-based adaptive tradeoff model (ArATM) proposed in ICDE.

The remaining part of this section is organized as follows: the first subsection provides a brief introduction of DE; the second subsection discusses the BDE algorithm; and in the end, the constraint-handling strategy used in the problem (i.e., ArATM) is presented.

3.1 Differential evolution

DE was originally proposed by Price and Storn in 1995 in a series of papers [31,50,51]. Since then, DE has gradually become one of the most successful branches of EA in continuous optimization and has been applied to many real-world problems with great success [52]. The procedures of DE are introduced as follows.

DE has only three hyperparameters: scale factor (F), crossover rate (C_r), and size of population (N_P). With the three hyperparameters properly configured, an initial population of N_P trial individuals are randomly generated. The trial individuals are denoted as $X_{i,g} = (x_{ij,g})$ for $i = 1, 2, \ldots, N_p$ and $j = 1, 2, \ldots, D$, where D is the dimension of the decision variable vector. The index g represents the generation number and starts from 1. The trial populations are adaptively improved over generations. At each iteration, a new generation replaces the old one through the processes of mutation, crossover, and selection.

In the mutation, several individuals are randomly chosen (sometimes the best individual is particularly chosen) to generate a mutant individual $V_{i,g+1} = (v_{ij,g+1})$ using a specific differential mutation operator. The differential mutation operator has several variants, and the majority of the variants can be represented as special cases of a generalized formula shown as follows [53]:

$$v_{i,j,g+1} = \lambda x_{bj,g} + (1 - \lambda)x_{r_1j,g} + \sum_{k=1}^{m} F\left(x_{r_{2k}j,g} - x_{r_{2k+1}j,g}\right) \tag{8}$$

where λ is a scalar taking values in the range from 0 to 1, b is the index of the best individual, m is a positive integer number, and r_i is a random positive integer number in the range from 1 to N_P. Note that $r_i \neq r_j$, given $i \neq j$. In some variants, $x_{r_1j,g}$ in the equation can be replaced with the current individual $x_{ij,g}$.

Subsequently, the crossover operation is applied to each dimension of each mutant individual $v_{ij,g+1}$ as well as the counterpart of the corresponding current individual $x_{ij,g}$ to generate the corresponding dimension of a trial individual $u_{ij,g+1}$. The crossover is introduced to boost the population diversity [53]. The commonly used crossover operation is the binomial crossover, which is shown as follows:

$$u_{ij,g+1} = \begin{cases} v_{ij,g+1} & \text{if } \text{rand}(0,1) \leq C_r \\ x_{ij,g} & \text{otherwise} \end{cases} \tag{9}$$

The new trial population $U_{i,g+1} = (u_{ij,g+1})$ is then evaluated, allowing the selection of the best individual between $U_{i,g+1}$ and $X_{i,g}$ for $i = 1, 2, \ldots, N_P$. The best individuals are collected and form the new population $X_{i,g+1}$, and the new population is passed toward the next iteration. The DE algorithms repeat these procedures iteratively as long as a stopping criterion is met. Then, the best individual in the last generation is presented as the solution.

The aforementioned algorithm is designed for continuous optimization problems. For problems with only binary variables, the approaches of DE can be different. The next subsection introduces the BDE algorithm that is used in this chapter.

3.2 Binary differential evolution

DE was originally developed to solve optimization problems with continuous decision variables. However, researchers have also applied DE to problems concerning only binary variables [37–39]. The algorithm used in this chapter is the BDE algorithm proposed by Gong and Tuson [38]. BDE utilizes the rigorous formal analysis to derive a DE variant for binary variables in a generic manner that inherits the true nature of DE for continuous variables [39]. The BDE algorithm considered herein is introduced as follows [39].

After the generation of the initial population, the mutant population $V_{i,g+1} = (v_{ij,g+1})$ is generated using the following operator: three mutually different indices r_1, r_2, and r_3 are randomly selected from 1 to N_P. Here, $x_{r_1j,g}$ is called the base vector. The individuals $x_{r_2j,g}$ and $x_{r_3j,g}$ together with a random number (i.e., rand $(0, 1)$) determine whether jth dimension of the $x_{r_1j,g}$ is flipped or not. The mutant operator can be described in the following equation:

$$v_{ij,g+1} = \begin{cases} 1 - x_{r_1 j,g} & if \quad x_{r_2 j,g} \neq x_{r_3 j,g} \quad and \ \mathrm{rand}(0,1) < F \\ x_{r_1 j,g} & otherwise \end{cases} \tag{10}$$

Then the crossover operation is performed to generate a new trial population. The crossover operation chosen here is the binomial crossover similar to Eq. (9). However, to ensure that the trial individual inherits at least one dimension from the mutant individual, random index $ridx \in \{1, ..., D\}$ is chosen and $u_{ij,g+1}$ is determined by:

$$u_{ij,g+1} = \begin{cases} v_{ij,g+1} & if \quad \mathrm{rand}(0,1) \leq C_r \quad or \quad j = ridx \\ x_{ij,g} & otherwise \end{cases} \tag{11}$$

At the end of each iteration, the selection is performed, so that the better individuals are chosen from $U_{i,g+1}$ and $X_{i,g}$ for $i = 1, 2, ..., N_P$. The procedure described above is for unconstrained optimization problems for binary variables. For CoPs, the constraint-handling strategy adopted herein is introduced in the next subsection.

3.3 Archiving-based adaptive tradeoff model (ArATM)

As the problem for the resilience enhancement is a CoP, a constraint-handling strategy is required to make sure the solution is in the feasible domain. In this study, ArATM in ICDE proposed by Jia et al. [36] is adopted to handle the constraints. ArATM is chosen herein, as it is able to appropriately make tradeoff between the objective function and the degree of constraint violation. Note that ArATM is only used in the selection, that is, the mutation and crossover described in the previous subsection are not affected. The procedures of ArATM are introduced as follows.

Let P_g denote the entire population of the current individuals $X_{i,g}$ and Q_g the entire population of the trial individuals $U_{i,g+1}$. H_g is the combined population of P_g and Q_g with the size of $2N_p$. All the individuals in H_g are denoted as $Y_{i,g}$. For CoP, the population may contain individuals that do not satisfy the constraints. Therefore, with regard to the combined population H_g, three cases may be encountered: (1) the infeasible case where all the individuals are infeasible, (2) the semifeasible case where both infeasible and feasible individuals exist, and (3) the feasible case where all the individuals are feasible.

For the infeasible case, the objective function $f(X)$ and the degree of constraint violation $G(X)$ are regarded as two objectives and are dealt with simultaneously. For an inequality constraint $g_i(X) \leq 0$, the constraint violation is defined as follows:

$$G_i(X) = \max\{0, g_i(X)\} \tag{12}$$

The algorithm of ArATM is presented as follows:

ALGORITHM 1 ARCHIVING-BASED ADAPTIVE TRADEOFF MODEL (ARATM).

Step (1) If archive A is not empty, *randsize* individuals are randomly selected from A and put into H_g. Here, *randsize* is an integer that is randomly generated between 0 and $|A|$;

Step (2) Set $A = \varnothing$;

Step (3) Set $P_{g+1} = \varnothing$;

Step (4) **While** $|P_{g+1}| < N_p$

Step (5) The nondominated individuals in H_g are identified depending on Pareto dominance;

Step (6) The nondominated individuals are sorted in ascending order based on their degree of constraint violations;

Step (7) The first half of the nondominated individuals are selected and stored into the population P_{g+1};

Step (8)   These selected nondominated individuals are removed from H_g;
Step (9) **End while**
Step (10) If $|P_{g+1}|>N_p$, delete the last $(|P_{g+1}|-N_p)$ individuals in P_{g+1} and store them into H_g;
Step (11) All the individuals in H_g are stored into A.

The hierarchical nondominated individual selection scheme with the individual archiving technique in this constraint-handling scheme motivates the population to move toward the feasible region and maintain a good diversity of the population simultaneously.

In the semiinfeasible case, information carried by certain infeasible individuals might be important to locate the optimal solution. Thus, it is reasonable to keep some of the useful infeasible individuals. Some feasible individuals with small objective function values and some infeasible individuals with both small degree of constraint violations and small objective function values are selected for the next generation. Let Z_1 denote the set of indices of all feasible individuals in H_g and Z_2 indicate the set of indices of all infeasible individuals in H_g. The objective function values for $Y_{i,g}$ are converted as follows:

$$f'(Y_{i,g}) = \begin{cases} f(Y_{i,g}) & i\in Z_1 \\ \max\left\{\varphi \times f(Y_{b,g}) + (1-\varphi)f(Y_{w,g}), f(Y_{i,g})\right\} & i\in Z_2 \end{cases} \tag{13}$$

where φ is the feasibility proportion of the combined population H_g, $Y_{b,g}$ is the feasible individual with the smallest objective function value, and $Y_{w,g}$ is the feasible individual with the largest objective function value. Then, a normalized objective function $f_{nor}'(Y_{i,g})$ is obtained as follows:

$$f'_{nor}(Y_{i,g}) = \frac{f'(Y_{i,g}) - \min_{j\in Z_1 \sqcup Z_2} f'(Y_{j,g})}{\max_{j\in Z_1 \sqcup Z_2} f'(Y_{j,g}) - \min_{j\in Z_1 \sqcup Z_2} f'(Y_{j,g})}, \quad i=1,2,\dots,2N_p \tag{14}$$

Meanwhile, the degree of constraint violation of each individual in H_g is normalized as:

$$G_{nor}(Y_{i,g}) = \begin{cases} 0 & i\in Z_1 \\ \dfrac{G(Y_{i,g}) - \min_{j\in Z_2} G(Y_{j,g})}{\max_{j\in Z_2} G(Y_{j,g}) - \min_{j\in Z_2} G(Y_{j,g})} & i\in Z_2 \end{cases} \tag{15}$$

Eventually, a final fitness function is obtained by combining $f_{nor}'(Y_{i,g})$ and $G_{nor}(Y_{i,g})$. N_p individuals with the smallest final fitness function value are added to P_{g+1}.

For the feasible case, N_p individuals with the least objective function values in H_g are selected to constitute P_{g+1} for the next generation.

4. Results

As mentioned in Section 2.2., the 7051 poles in the PDN are categorized into 15 clusters. The clustering here is facilitated by a risk-based index called modified expected outage reduction (MEOR). The details about this index can be found in [8]. The poles are ranked based on MEOR and then classified into 15 clusters, where clusters 1 and 15 contain the pole with the lowest and highest MEORs, respectively. It is worth noting that for utility poles that have the same age, replacing the poles with higher MEOR can lead to a higher increase in the resilience of the PDN. After clustering, the BICDE algorithm is used to solve the optimization model presented in Eq. (7). All computations are performed using Python on a personal computer equipped with an Intel Core i7-6700 CPU with a core clock of 3.40 GHz and 16 GB of RAM. On average, the algorithm converges after about 1250 generations. The total computational time until convergence is approximately 5 h. The solution of this problem is illustrated in Fig. 1. It can be observed from Fig. 1 that 30 clusters are replaced during the planning horizon and the maximum number of cluster replacements per period is 2. It is also shown that the duration between two subsequent replacements of a cluster is equal to or greater than 8 periods. Therefore, all three constraints are satisfied. Although the constraint on the time between two subsequent cluster replacements is 8 periods in most cases, the optimal solution recommends replacing a new cluster after 10 periods. This trend occurs because there is a tradeoff between reducing the time between two subsequent replacements to enhance the resilience of the PDN over a short period and distributing cluster replacements over the planning horizon to maintain the PDN resilient over the entire planning horizon. According to Fig. 1, the BICDE-based planning recommends replacing three clusters with the highest MEOR three times over the entire planning horizon, whereas one replacement is recommended for three clusters with the lowest MEOR. This observation implies the capability of MEOR to properly cluster the poles.

The performance of the solution obtained by BICDE is compared with the performance of the NESC strategy in terms of the life-cycle hurricane resilience of the PDN. This comparison is presented in Fig. 2. Observing the expected resilience of the PDN over the extended planning horizon, it is evident that the BICDE-based strategy outperforms the NESC strategy. According to Fig. 2, except for a few years at the beginning of the planning horizon, the BICDE significantly increases the resilience of the PDN. The NESC strategy results in a minimum resilience of 99.08% over the entire planning horizon; however, applying the proposed BICDE-based strategy increases the minimum resilience to 99.28%.

The differences between the expected resilience of the BICDE-based strategy and the NESC strategy are shown in Fig. 3. Although the maximum difference between the expected resilience of the strategies is around 0.5%, such enhancements in the expected annual resilience of PDNs can lead to saving millions of dollars. For example, according to a loss estimation by Ouyang and Dueñas-Osorio [54], for an electric power system in Harris County, a 0.038% decrease in the expected annual resilience can

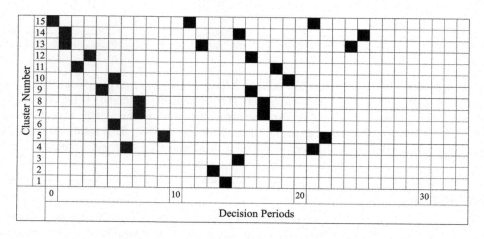

FIG. 1

Optimal preventive maintenance strategy as the solution of BICDE.

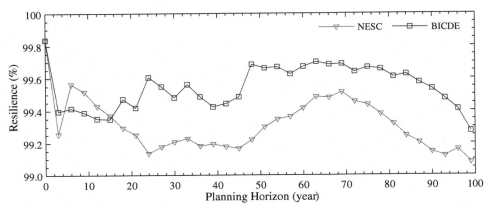

FIG. 2

Impacts of preventive maintenance strategies on the resilience of the PDN.

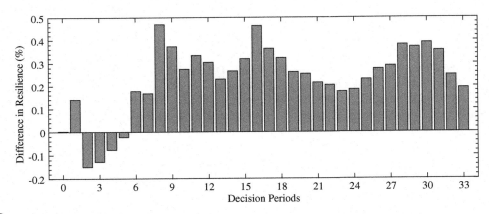

FIG. 3

Difference between the expected resilience of the PDN maintained by the BICDE-based strategy and the NESC strategy.

incur annual economic losses as high as $83 million dollars. Therefore, even marginal improvements in the expected resilience are significantly important. The mean of the difference between the expected annual resilience of the strategies is 0.231% and the cumulative improvement in the expected resilience of the PDN is 23.1% over the 100-year period of the planning horizon. This result indicates that the integration of optimization in identifying the preventive maintenance strategy is crucial.

5. Conclusions

In this chapter, an optimization model is presented to enhance the resilience of a large-scale aging power distribution network (PDN) that is susceptible to gradual deterioration as well as multiple stochastic occurrences of hurricane events. This optimization model is a nonlinear constrained problem with binary decision variables for preventive maintenance actions. To solve the constrained optimization problem, the BICDE algorithm is implemented via the integration of a binary differential evolutionary (BDE) algorithm and the improved $(\mu+\lambda)$-constrained differential evolution (ICDE). The optimal preventive maintenance strategy obtained by solving the optimization model is compared to the strength-based strategy set by National Electric Safety Code (NESC). The results indicate that the BICDE-based strategy on average improves the expected cumulative resilience of the PDN by 23.1% over a planning horizon of 100 years compared to the NESC strategy, which leads to mitigation of the hurricane-induced economic losses by millions of dollars per year.

References

[1] E.S. Blake, D.A. Zelinsky, National Hurricane center tropical cyclone report: Hurricane Harvey, AL092017, National Oceanic and Atmospheric Administration, 2017.

[2] M. Aghababaei, M. Koliou, S.G. Paal, Performance assessment of building infrastructure impacted by the 2017 Hurricane Harvey in the port Aransas Region, J. Perform. Constr. Facil. 32 (5) (2018) 04018069.

[3] S. Zamanian, B. Terranova, A. Shafieezadeh, Significant variables affecting the performance of concrete panels impacted by wind-borne projectiles: a global sensitivity analysis, Int. J. Impact Eng. 144 (2020) 103650.

[4] EPRI, Electric Power System Resiliency: Challenges and Opportunities, Palo Alto, CA, USA, 3002007376, 2016.

[5] M. Panteli, P. Mancarella, Influence of extreme weather and climate change on the resilience of power systems: impacts and possible mitigation strategies, Electr. Pow. Syst. Res. 127 (2015) 259–270.

[6] L. Ceferino, H.A. Ibrahim, S.J. Hormozabad, T. Kijewski-Correa, S.F. Pikington, D. Robertson, Event briefing, in: StEER—Hurricane Zeta, DesignSafe-CI, 2020, https://doi.org/10.17603/ds2-67r3-2y51.

[7] Executive Office of the President, Economic benefits of increasing electric grid resilience to weather outzages, in: IEEE USA Books & eBooks, 2013. [Online]. Available https://www.energy.gov/sites/prod/files/2013/08/f2/Grid%20Resiliency%20Report_FINAL.pdf.

[8] N.L. Dehghani, A.B. Jeddi, A. Shafieezadeh, Intelligent hurricane resilience enhancement of power distribution systems via deep reinforcement learning, Appl. Energy 285 (2021) 116355.

[9] S. Zamanian, M. Rahimi, A. Shafieezadeh, Resilience of sewer networks to extreme weather hazards: past experiences and an assessment framework, in: Pipelines 2020, American Society of Civil Engineers, Reston, VA, 2020, pp. 50–59.

[10] A. Shafieezadeh, L.I. Burden, Scenario-based resilience assessment framework for critical infrastructure systems: case study for seismic resilience of seaports, Reliab. Eng. Syst. Saf. 132 (2014) 207–219.

[11] S. Moradi, V. Vasandani, B.S. Student, A. Nejat, A review of resilience variables in the context of disasters, J. Emergency Manage. 17 (5) (2019) 403–432.

[12] W. Yuan, J. Wang, F. Qiu, C. Chen, C. Kang, B. Zeng, Robust optimization-based resilient distribution network planning against natural disasters, IEEE Trans. Smart Grid 7 (6) (2016) 2817–2826.

[13] S. Ma, B. Chen, Z. Wang, Resilience enhancement strategy for distribution systems under extreme weather events, IEEE Trans. Smart Grid 9 (2) (2016) 1442–1451.

[14] B. Farahi, M.R. Esfahani, J. Sabzi, Experimental investigation on the behavior of reinforced concrete beams retrofitted with NSM-SMA/FRP, Amirkabir J. Civil Eng. 51 (4) (2018), https://doi.org/10.22060/mej.2017.503.

[15] S. Muzenski, I. Flores-Vivian, B. Farahi, K. Sobolev, Towards ultrahigh performance concrete produced with aluminum oxide nanofibers and reduced quantities of silica fume, Nanomaterials 10 (11) (2020) 2291.

[16] National Electrical Safety Code® (NESC®), ANSI/IEEE Standard, 2017.

[17] T. N. Bowmer, n.d."National Electrical Safety Code (NESC) update," Presented at the ATIS Protection Engineers Group Conference, Dallas, Texas, USA, 1207, [Online]. Available: https://peg.atis.org/wp-content/uploads/sites/16/2018/08/NESC_Update_TrevorBowmer.pdf.

[18] E. Fereshtehnejad, A. Shafieezadeh, A multi-type multi-occurrence hazard lifecycle cost analysis framework for infrastructure management decision making, Eng. Struct. 167 (2018) 504–517.

[19] N.L. Dehghani, A. Shafieezadeh, Probabilistic sustainability assessment of bridges subjected to multi-occurrence hazards, in: International Conference on Sustainable Infrastructure 2019: Leading Resilient Communities through the 21st Century, Los Angeles, CA, 2019, pp. 555–565.

[20] N.L. Dehghani, E. Fereshtehnejad, A. Shafieezadeh, A Markovian approach to infrastructure life-cycle analysis: modeling the interplay of hazard effects and recovery, Earthq. Eng. Struct. Dyn. (2020). https://doi.org/10.1002/eqe.3359.

[21] M. Aghababaei, M. Mahsuli, Detailed seismic risk analysis of buildings using structural reliability methods, Probab. Eng. Mech. 53 (2018) 23–38.

[22] E. Fereshtehnejad, A. Shafieezadeh, Multiple hazard incidents lifecycle cost assessment of structural systems considering state-dependent repair times and fragility curves, Earthq. Eng. Struct. Dyn. 45 (14) (2016) 2327–2347.

[23] M. Sheibani, G. Ou, S. Zhe, Rapid seismic risk assessment of structures with gaussian process regression, in: Dynamic Substructures, vol. 4, Springer, 2020, pp. 159–165.

[24] M. Rahimi, N.L. Dehghani, A. Shafieezadeh, Probabilistic lifecycle cost analysis of levees against backward Erosion, in: International Conference on Sustainable Infrastructure 2019: Leading Resilient Communities through the 21st Century, Los Angeles, CA, 2019, pp. 566–574.

[25] Y.M. Darestani, K. Sanny, A. Shafieezadeh, E. Fereshtehnejad, Life cycle resilience quantification and enhancement of power distribution systems: a risk-based approach, Struct. Saf. 90 (2021) 102075.

[26] A.M. Salman, Y. Li, M.G. Stewart, Evaluating system reliability and targeted hardening strategies of power distribution systems subjected to hurricanes, Reliab. Eng. Syst. Saf. 144 (2015) 319–333.

[27] N.L. Dehghani, Y.M. Darestani, A. Shafieezadeh, Optimal life-cycle resilience enhancement of aging power distribution systems: a MINLP-based preventive maintenance planning, IEEE Access 8 (2020) 22324–22334.

[28] J.H. Holland, Genetic algorithms, Sci. Am. 267 (1) (1992) 66–73.

[29] J.R. Koza, R. Poli, Genetic programming, in: E.K. Burke, G. Kendall (Eds.), Search Methodologies: Introductory Tutorials in Optimization and Decision Support Techniques, Springer US, Boston, MA, 2005, pp. 127–164.

[30] H.-G. Beyer, H.-P. Schwefel, Evolution strategies—a comprehensive introduction, Nat. Comput. 1 (1) (Mar. 2002) 3–52, https://doi.org/10.1023/A:1015059928466.

[31] R. Storn, K. Price, Differential evolution—a simple and efficient heuristic for global optimization over continuous spaces, J. Glob. Optim. 11 (4) (Dec 1997) 341–359, https://doi.org/10.1023/A:1008202821328.

[32] N. Karaboga, B. Cetinkaya, Performance comparison of genetic and differential evolution algorithms for digital FIR filter design, in: Advances in Information Systems, Berlin, Heidelberg, 2005, pp. 482–488, https://doi.org/10.1007/978-3-540-30198-1_49.

[33] E. Mezura-Montes, J. Velazquez-Reyes, C.A. Coello Coello, Modified differential evolution for constrained optimization, in: 2006 IEEE International Conference on Evolutionary Computation, Jul 2006, pp. 25–32, https://doi.org/10.1109/CEC.2006.1688286.

[34] E. Mezura-Montes, M.E. Miranda-Varela, R. del Carmen Gómez-Ramón, Differential evolution in constrained numerical optimization: an empirical study, Inform. Sci. 180 (22) (Nov. 2010) 4223–4262, https://doi.org/10.1016/j.ins.2010.07.023.

[35] Y. Wang, Z. Cai, Constrained evolutionary optimization by means of $(\mu + \lambda)$-differential evolution and improved adaptive trade-off model, Evol. Comput. 19 (2) (Jun 2011) 249–285, https://doi.org/10.1162/EVCO_a_00024.

[36] G. Jia, Y. Wang, Z. Cai, Y. Jin, An improved $(\mu+\lambda)$-constrained differential evolution for constrained optimization, Inform. Sci. 222 (Feb. 2013) 302–322, https://doi.org/10.1016/j.ins.2012.01.017.

[37] G. Pampara, A.P. Engelbrecht, N. Franken, Binary differential evolution, in: 2006 IEEE International Conference on Evolutionary Computation, Jul 2006, pp. 1873–1879, https://doi.org/10.1109/CEC.2006.1688535.

[38] T. Gong, A.L. Tuson, Differential evolution for binary encoding, in: Soft Computing in Industrial Applications, 2007, pp. 251–262, https://doi.org/10.1007/978-3-540-70706-6_24. Berlin, Heidelberg.

[39] B. Doerr, W. Zheng, Working principles of binary differential evolution, Theor. Comput. Sci. 801 (Jan. 2020) 110–142, https://doi.org/10.1016/j.tcs.2019.08.025.

[40] A.P. Engelbrecht, G. Pampara, Binary differential evolution strategies, in: 2007 IEEE Congress on Evolutionary Computation, Sep 2007, pp. 1942–1947, https://doi.org/10.1109/CEC.2007.4424711.

[41] H. Su, Y. Yang, Quantum-inspired differential evolution for binary optimization, in: 2008 Fourth International Conference on Natural Computation, vol. 1, Oct 2008, pp. 341–346, https://doi.org/10.1109/ICNC.2008.607.

[42] C. Peng, L. Jian, L. Zhiming, Solving 0–1 knapsack problems by a discrete binary version of differential evolution, in: 2008 Second International Symposium on Intelligent Information Technology Application, vol. 2, Dec 2008, pp. 513–516, https://doi.org/10.1109/IITA.2008.538.

[43] C. Deng, B. Zhao, Y. Yang, A. Deng, Novel binary differential evolution algorithm for discrete optimization, in: 2009 Fifth International Conference on Natural Computation, vol. 4, Aug 2009, pp. 346–349, https://doi.org/10.1109/ICNC.2009.188.

[44] X. He, Q. Zhang, N. Sun, Y. Dong, Feature selection with discrete binary differential evolution, in: 2009 International Conference on Artificial Intelligence and Computational Intelligence, vol. 4, Nov 2009, pp. 327–330, https://doi.org/10.1109/AICI.2009.438.

[45] Y. Chen, W. Xie, X. Zou, A binary differential evolution algorithm learning from explored solutions, Neurocomputing 149 (2015) 1038–1047, https://doi.org/10.1016/j.neucom.2014.07.030.

[46] F. Kiessling, P. Nefzger, J.F. Nolasco, U. Kaintzyk, Overhead Power Lines: Planning, Design, Construction, Springer, 2014.

[47] A. Shafieezadeh, P.U. Onyewuchi, M.M. Begovic, R. DesRoches, Fragility assessment of wood poles in power distribution networks against extreme wind hazards, in: ATC & SEI Conference on Advances in Hurricane Engineering: Learning from Our Past, Miami, FL, American Society of Civil Engineers, 2013, pp. 851–861.

[48] A. Shafieezadeh, U.P. Onyewuchi, M.M. Begovic, R. DesRoches, Age-dependent fragility models of utility wood poles in power distribution networks against extreme wind hazards, IEEE Trans. Power Delivery 29 (1) (2013) 131–139.

[49] Y.M. Darestani, A. Shafieezadeh, Multi-dimensional wind fragility functions for wood utility poles, Eng. Struct. 183 (2019) 937–948.

[50] K.V. Price, Differential evolution: a fast and simple numerical optimizer, in: Proceedings of North American Fuzzy Information Processing, Jun 1996, pp. 524–527, https://doi.org/10.1109/NAFIPS.1996.534790.

[51] R. Storn, On the usage of differential evolution for function optimization, in: Proceedings of North American Fuzzy Information Processing, Jun 1996, pp. 519–523, https://doi.org/10.1109/NAFIPS.1996.534789.

[52] S. Das, S.S. Mullick, P.N. Suganthan, Recent advances in differential evolution—an updated survey, Swarm Evol. Comput. 27 (Apr. 2016) 1–30, https://doi.org/10.1016/j.swevo.2016.01.004.

[53] K.R. Opara, J. Arabas, Differential evolution: a survey of theoretical analyses, Swarm Evol. Comput. 44 (2019) 546–558, https://doi.org/10.1016/j.swevo.2018.06.010.

[54] M. Ouyang, L. Duenas-Osorio, Multi-dimensional hurricane resilience assessment of electric power systems, Struct. Saf. 48 (2014) 15–24.

Application of nature-inspired computing paradigms in optimal design of structural engineering problems—a review

Amit Kumar

Department of Information Technology, Rajkiya Engineering College, Ambedkar Nagar, Akbarpur, Uttar Pradesh, India

1. Introduction

Engineers face trade-offs between different product attributes such as: cost, weight, manufacturing capacity, quality, and efficiency during product design and production. Their goal is to achieve the best overall design by making the correct choices, but there should be no concessions on crucial qualities such as protection. Design optimization requires the use of computational optimization techniques to design material-efficient or cost-effective systems that improve the performance and quality of the material application while minimizing the cost of the life cycle. There may be a number of uncertainties in an engineering design problem. Typical examples of such uncertainty include the divergence of real loads, structural properties, geometry, etc. from the values assumed during the design process. These complexities may have a negative impact on performance. Hence, robust and reliability-based design optimization techniques that ensure sensitivity with respect to limited uncertainties should be used. Structural architecture optimization issues are usually expressed as a nonlinear programming concern involving continuous, binary, discrete, and integer variables. Structural architecture optimization strategies that aim to improve or locate the right mechanical structures are divided into three categories: scale optimization, form optimization, and topology optimization. They are applied to the construction of load-bearing systems, structural elements, or structural materials under static or dynamic loading in the absence or existence of uncertainties. The goal of the design optimization process is to find the optimum value of the parameters that yield the optimum value of the given objective function. A general constrained optimization problem can be described as:

$$\max_{x_i \in R} f(x_1, x_2, x_3, ..., x_n)$$

Subject to :

$$g_1(x_1, ..., x_n) \le b_1, ..., g_k(x_1, ..., x_n) \le b_k,$$

$$h_1(x_1, ..., x_n) = c_1, ..., h_m(x_1, ..., x_n) = c_m.$$

Nature-Inspired Computing Paradigms in Systems. https://doi.org/10.1016/B978-0-12-823749-6.00010-6

where function $f(x)$ is the objective function. $g(x)$ and $h(x)$ represent the k inequality and m equality constraints, respectively.

The constrained optimization problem differs from the normal unrestricted optimization problem since here the maximum value of $f(x)$ has to be found over the points that satisfy the constraints. The objective function may include several constraints depending on the problem. Structural engineering architecture challenges are usually nonlinear and require a vast number of mixed decision variables and constraints. Furthermore, the effect of these decision variables on objective function is significant. The presence of two types of constraints—equalities and inequalities—makes it difficult to find the feasible solution. Such problems cannot be addressed by the classical method [1]. The requirement of the designer is to find global optimal value; however, the classical methods compute only local optima, so they are not efficient. In the literature, the most generic approach for handling constraints is to employ penalty functions. However, these penalty functions involve a large number of parameters. The suitable combinations of these parameters should be found to make a balance between the objective and penalty functions by making adjustments in their values. In the literature, researchers have proposed various approaches to address these design optimization problems: successive linear approximation approach [2], Davidson-Fletcher-Powell penalty function method, simplex method with penalty function, Richardson's random method, augmented multiplier-based method [3], numerical optimization technique called a constraint correction at the constraint cost [4], nonlinear branch and bound algorithms based on integer programming [5], etc. These classical methods are able to find the global optimum for simple and ideal models; however, their crucial deficiency is revealed when applied to complex real-world engineering optimization problems. Therefore, intelligent methods are required for addressing constrained design problems efficiently. In [6], approaches to address optimization problems were divided into two categories: deterministic and heuristic approaches. Deterministic methods like linear programming, nonlinear programming, and mixed-integer nonlinear programming are general techniques for problem-solving optimization focused on the analytical properties of the problem. When applied to nonconvex or large-scale optimization problems, however, deterministic methods cannot offer a globally optimal solution within a rational timeframe. Metaheuristic methods have been shown to be more stable and effective in relation to certain problems. They address the disadvantages and limitations encountered by conventional numerical approaches and reduce the computing time required to solve the optimization problem [7]. A metaheuristic is a problem-independent methodology applied to a wide variety of problems. This is an iterative approach that directs a subordinate heuristic by integrating intelligently separate ideas for discovery and utilization of the search space. The inspiration for metaheuristic algorithms stems from natural phenomena. In nature-inspired metaheuristic algorithms, a population of search agents explore the search space to ensure greater exploration to find global optima. Genetic algorithm [8] and simulated annealing [9] are two of the primitive nature-inspired metaheuristics. Over the last two decades, there has been an explosion of novel nature-inspired metaheuristics due to their flexibility and effectiveness.

2. Nature-inspired algorithms

Mother Nature is the greatest of all innovators. Nature is an incessant source of inspiration that has given cues to the scientific community to derive some of the most effective design optimization methods in technology innovation. Nature-inspired algorithms (NIAs) have successfully handled numerous real-world difficult and complicated optimization problems. These techniques learn from the way in which real biological systems deal with real-world situations. NIAs simulate various biological systems, such as the human brain, a colony of ants, human immune systems, etc. Nature-based meta-heuristic algorithms are inspired by swarm intelligence, biological processes, and physical and chemical systems.

2.1 Swarm intelligence algorithms

A significant number of insects and other minor animals, such as flies, bees, fish, etc., are typically arranged in hierarchies in nature. These social insects demonstrate a remarkable ability to solve complicated problems, such as forming their nest or determining the shortest path between their nest and the food supply. In these organisms, although each individual agent has limited responses, the agents all together exhibit fascinating behavior and obvious traits of intelligence. For example, when swimming carelessly, fish retain a greater reciprocal distance, while they come together in very dense groups in the face of predators. The members of the group react collectively to external attacks to protect the personal dignity of each member of the group. The term "swarm" is used for a large number of insects or other small creatures that carry out group behavior, such as bees, social wasps, termites, ants, or an aggregation of animals or birds such as fish, cats, dogs, etc. [10]. The individual agents of these swarms operate without oversight; because of their perception of the neighborhood, each of these agents has a stochastic behavior. The swarm is able to change its current form rapidly by breaking into smaller parts and then reuniting again when there is no danger. This behavior in natural processes has stimulated scientific interest about the fundamental laws that cause this behavior. Systems where such collective phenomena occur prepare the ground for the development of swarm intelligence (SI) [11]. Swarm intelligence is an artificial intelligence branch that studies the collective actions and emerging properties of complex, self-organized, socially structured, decentralized systems. SI aims to simulate the behavior of any loosely structured collection of interacting agents. Emergent behavior is only attainable through local communications among system constituents and cannot be achieved by any individual component of the system by acting unaided [12]. The SI system is capable of operating in a synchronized fashion without any coordinator or external controller. In a swarm, while each agent has a very small field of operation with no central influence, the aggregated activity of the whole swarm shows characteristics of intelligence (i.e., the ability to respond to environmental changes and decision-making capability). SI techniques are used to design intelligent systems that replace control, preprogramming, and centralization with autonomy, emergence, and distributiveness. Erratic and irregular behavior of social insects does not distract them from the targeted goal. Rather, it enables them to discover and explore in addition to exploiting the environment to achieve their goal. Self-organization feeds itself on failures to provide agents with resilience (i.e., agents can respond to an evolving environment) and robustness (i.e., the community can still execute its activities, even though one or two people fail). The indirect communication by which the individuals interact with each other depicts a complex group behavior. Indeed, the appearance of such collective behavior out of simple indirect way of communication is one of the biggest motivating factors of SI. SI techniques differ from the traditional approaches by being flexible and robust with decentralized control. Solutions are emergent rather than predefined and preprogrammed. Examples of structures studied by SI include colonies of ants, bees, and termites; schools of fish; flocks of birds; herds of land animals, etc. Despite their physical or structural variations, these networks share characteristics based on the five fundamental concepts of SI: proximity, quality, plurality of responses, stability, and adaptability. Natural intelligent swarms solve many problems in nature like finding food sources, division of labor among nest mates, building nests, etc. For example, ants find shortest paths between their nest and the food source, even if subjected to a varying environment or despite the failure of individual ants via stigmergy [13]. It is a type of indirect communication that is mediated by environmental change. When ants search for food, they leave behind pheromones, a substance that attracts other ants. Similarly, bees searching for a new hive location present another case. Bees use a "dance" to communicate regarding the characteristics of food sources. Numerous scouts search for prospective areas; upon their return, they perform a distinctive "waggle dance" [14]that communicates in code the path to the newly discovered site. The speed of the bee's movements indicates its enthusiasm for the prospective location. When several scouts select the same location, the entire swarm moves. The problems that natural intelligent swarms address in nature have important counterparts in many real-world engineering fields. Biologists and environmental scientists actively mimic the behavior of natural swarms in novel numerical optimization techniques. As a result, SI transpires all the time as a more important research area for researchers from engineering, economics, bioinformatics, operations research, and many other disciplines. Through mimicking nature-inspired swarming behavior in computing methodologies, strategies arise for hard optimization problems that are stable, scalable, and easily distributed. Initially, the two key approaches to SI were: ant colony optimization based on an ant colony [15] and particle swarm optimization described by and based on bird flocking [16]. Both methods have been widely applied to a variety of real-world challenges in various fields. In recent years, several new SI algorithms have been successfully applied to the issue of structural architecture.

2.2 Bioinspired algorithms

Biology is an area of research that attempts to discover the rules of nature that underlie the form and actions of living organisms. [17]. It is a baffling source of inspiration for the design and creation of intelligent algorithms that can be used in unfamiliar and evolving conditions. Bioinspired artificial intelligence is thus inspired by the processes of natural life systems and a wider range of biological structures capable of autonomous self-organization. Examples of bioinspired artificial intelligence include behavior-based robots, artificial neural networks, evolutionary computing and evolutionary electronics, and immune systems—to list just a handful. Any bioinspired algorithm consists of the following three steps: choosing an acceptable representation of the problem, determining the superiority of the solution through a fitness function, and voicing new operators with a view to create a new set of solutions [18]. Biologically influenced computation is a branch of nature-inspired computing. While the components of biological systems respond slowly, they nevertheless carry out far higher-level operations. These networks assemble and evolve on their own, allowing even higher densities of interconnection to be reached. Biological processes are not designed for implementation, but they are normal. The main divisions in bioinspired algorithms involve evolution-based algorithms, ecology-based algorithms, and other SI-based algorithms. These are inspired by natural evolution, natural ecosystems, and collective behavior in animals, respectively [18]. The most popular and established algorithms among bioinspired algorithms are evolutionary algorithms viz. genetic algorithm (GA) [19], genetic programming (GP) [20], differential evolution (DE) [21], evolutionary strategy (ES), and the most recent, paddy field algorithm (PFA). These are based on biological evolution in nature. Furthermore, natural ecosystems impart great inspiration for designing algorithms to solve difficult engineering and computer science problems.

2.3 Physics- and chemistry-based algorithms

Some metaheuristic optimization algorithms are inspired by certain physical and chemical processes. These algorithms imitate physical and/or chemical principles like electrical charges, gravity, river structures, etc. These physics- and chemistry-based algorithms may or may not belong to the set of bioinspired algorithms. Simulated annealing [9] and Harmony Search [22] are two of the popular algorithms developed initially. Refs. [23, 24] proposed a quantum computing system inspired by quantum mechanics. With this, these works also proposed quantum-inspired algorithms, which are physics-based algorithms.

3. Nature-inspired metaheuristics in optimal design of structural engineering problems

Nature-inspired techniques are utilized for the modern intelligent solution approach. These techniques are very efficient in developing effective algorithms in modern artificial intelligence research. These techniques can also be combined to form hybrid approaches. Nature-inspired algorithms can be categorized on the basis of their source of inspiration (i.e., swarm-based, bioinspired, physics and chemistry). A few algorithms from each of these variants have proved to be very effective tools to solve the optimal design problem. These are discussed in the next subsection.

3.1 SI algorithms in optimal design of structural engineering problems

The action of certain collective living organisms, such as ants, termites, birds, and fish, is the basis for SI algorithms. The two mainstreams in SI, ant colony optimization (ACO) and particle swarm optimization (PSO), have been used in a variety of experiments to solve optimization problems over the last decades. A variety of new SI algorithms have appeared in recent years. The famous SI techniques used to solve the optimum design problem are as follows:

- *PSO-based approaches*: In [25], a PSO algorithm was used to address mixed-integer design optimization problems. PSO has demonstrated positive results in the fields of structural design optimization [26, 27] and topology optimization [26]. In [28], a PSO algorithm was applied to three classic nonconvex truss structural optimization examples where it demonstrated its efficacy and constraint handling potential. In [29], PSO was used to optimize the truss weight. In [30], PSO was used to assess the optimum reliability-based configuration of truss structures. In [31], the PSO approach was applied to reinforce concrete beam design according to AS 360000. In [32], a PSO algorithm with time-varying acceleration coefficients was used to minimize the cost design of concrete slabs. In [33], modified PSO was employed to optimize the design of spread footing and retaining walls. In [34], PSO was used to optimize the design of unbraced steel frames to Load and Resistance Factor Design-American Institute of Steel Construction (LRFD-AISC). In [35], a virtual tool for minimum cost design of a wind turbine tower with ring stiffeners was developed in MATLAB using PSO.

- *ACO-based approaches*: It was shown in [36] that the ACO algorithm is a valuable and theoretically feasible optimization technique for the discrete-variable optimal structural configuration of a 25-bar space truss when used for weight minimization. The discrete configuration variables in this application were the cross-sectional areas of the bars. In [37], an ACO algorithm was employed for the discrete optimization of steel frames. The improved ACO algorithm for the design of planar steel frames was introduced in [38]. In [39], ACO methodology was applied to arrive at the optimal design of concrete retaining walls. ACO's application for cost optimization of the composite floor system was introduced in [40] on the basis of the load and resistance factor design requirements of AISC. In [41], the ACO algorithm was used for achieving an optimal layout of multispan reinforced concrete beams of bridge for minimizing the overall cost. In [42], ACO was used to determine the optimum cross-section of the tunnel structures.
- *Firefly algorithm (FA)-based approaches*: In [43], an FA was used to resolve the six classical problems of structural optimization concerning both discrete and continuous variables: pressure vessel, welded beam, reinforced concrete beam, helical compression spring, stepped cantilever beam, and the problem of car side effect or the car side impact problem. In [44], FA was used to solve and optimize the truss structure for a 10-bar plane truss, 17-bar plane truss, 25-bar space truss, and 72-bar space truss. In [45], an adaptive FA was used for the discrete design optimization of space steel frames for a four storeys, 132-member space frame and an eight-storey, 1024-member space frame. In [46], the sequential quadratic programming (SQP) was combined with a new hybrid firefly algorithm for the optimal design of reinforced concrete foundations.
- *Bat algorithm (BA)-based approaches*: The capacity of the BA was investigated in [47] to minimize the weight of three functional truss systems subject to constraints of weight, stiffness, and displacement. In [48], a BA was applied to achieve the optimum design of reinforced concrete plane moment frames. In [49], a BA was proposed to optimize the weight of steel frames subjected to stress, stability, nodal displacement, and drift constraints. The improved BA was used in [50] to maximize the scale of the skeletal structures consisting of truss and frame structures.
- *Artificial bee colony (ABC)-based approaches*: In [51], an ABC algorithm was proposed for solving structural engineering design optimization problems. In [52], the ABC algorithm was used to reduce the weight of truss systems for five instances of fixed geometry that fulfilled all structural criteria imposed by design codes. In [53], the ABC algorithm was used to optimize four distinct skeletal structures. In [54], the ABC algorithm was used to achieve an optimal configuration for continuous beams of reinforced concrete. In [55], the ABC algorithm was employed to optimize the real size steel frame. In [56], the reliability and efficiency of the ABC algorithm was used for locating the critical slip circle in the slope stability analysis for six benchmark examples.
- *Grey wolf optimizer (GWO)-based approach*: In [57], GWO was suggested and the high efficiency of the algorithm in uncertain, demanding search spaces was checked by applying it to three constrained engineering design problems: tension/compression spring, welded beam, and pressure vessel design.
- *Dragonfly algorithm (DA)-based approach*: In [58], the DA was proposed and used for designing a real propeller for submarines.
- *Moth-flame optimization (MFO)-based approach*: In [59], MFO algorithm was proposed and its effectiveness was tested by applying it to seven classical engineering test problems: gear train

design, welded beam design, pressure vessel design, three-bar truss design, pressure vessel design, I-beam design cantilever design, and tension/compression spring design.

- *Whale optimization algorithm (WOA)-based approach*: In [60], the WOA was suggested and extended to six structural engineering problems: welded beam design, tension/compression spring design, pressure vessel design, 15-bar truss design, 25-bar truss design, and 52-bar truss design. These design problems have different limitations, so the death penalty function is used as a constraint handling method that assigns a high objective value (in case of minimization).
- *Salp swarm algorithm (SSA)-based approach*: In [61], the SSA and its multiobjective version were proposed. These were applied to solve the challenging and computationally expensive five classical engineering design problems: welded beam design, three-bar truss design, cantilever beam design, I-beam design, tension/compression spring design, and airfoil design for aero vehicles.
- *Grasshopper optimization algorithm (GOA)-based approach*: In [62], the GOA was suggested and the applicability of this algorithm was illustrated by using it to find the optimum form of a 52-bar truss, 3-bar truss, and cantilever beam.
- *Crow search algorithm (CSA)-based approaches*: In [63], the CSA was introduced with the goal of seeking optimal solutions to structural engineering problems such as pressure vessel design, welded beam design, and tension/compression string design.

3.2 Bioinspired algorithms in optimal design of structural engineering problems

Evolutionary algorithms are the most general and influential biologically inspired algorithms. They are inspired by natural evolution. These algorithms have been applied to an impressive variety of optimization problems. The DE, GA, GP, ES, and PFA are the most popular evolutionary algorithms that have been applied successfully by researches to various optimization problems. Biological processes are constrained optimization processes that make use of several random choices. In recent years, several new bioinspired algorithms that are inspired by these biological processes have emerged. The popular bioinspired techniques used to solve optimal design problem are as follows:

- *GA-based approaches*: In [64], GA was employed for solving mixed-integer engineering design optimization problems. In [65], the concept of GA was used for a 3-bar truss problem. In [66], an optimization technique based on GA was presented for the layout of truss structures. In [67], GA was used for optimal design of space truss structures. In [68], GA was used in discrete optimization of steel truss roofs. In [69], a global search method was presented for topology optimization of truss structures using GA. In [70], a fuzzy controlled GA-based search technique was presented.
- *DE-based approaches*: An updated DE algorithm was suggested in [71] to solve engineering design problems. In this algorithm, parameters based on viability and a diversity process were used to preserve an unfeasible solution.

3.3 Physics- and chemistry-based algorithms in optimal design of structural engineering problems

Researchers have proposed numerous optimization algorithms that are inspired by various fields of physics, such as quantum theory, electrostatics, electromagnetism, Newton's Gravitational Laws, and Laws of Motion. Quantum computation is the most attractive field in physics that draws the focus of science to quantum-based algorithms. There is substantial literature on the hybridization between quantum computation and the biological phenomena, owing to the parallel existence of quantum computing. Newton's Gravitational Laws and Laws of Motion are also common fields. The common physics- and chemistry-based techniques used to solve design optimization problems are as follows:

- *Simulated annealing (SA)-based approaches*: In [72], a hybrid approach of SA and GA was proposed for structural optimization problems.
- *Quantum-behaved PSO (QBSO)-based approaches*: In [73], a QBPSO approach that involved mutation operator with Gaussian probability distribution was presented.
- *Harmony search (HS)-based approaches*: In [7], an HS algorithm was used to address continuous engineering optimization.

4. Discussion

One of the most important advantages of nature-inspired algorithms is that these algorithms do not use gradients to explore and manipulate the problem's search area. Instead of conveniently distinguishing near-optimal solutions, they combine natural pattern laws and randomness. Obviously, their success can be due to several reasons, and one main explanation is that these algorithms are quick, scalable, powerful, and highly adjustable. In addition, from the implementation point of view, it is very simple to implement these algorithms in any programming language. As a result, these algorithms have been extended to a wide variety of concerns in real-world implementations. Optimization of design in civil engineering is essentially structural optimization since the key tasks for the design of systems are to optimize the output index and minimize costs, according to complex, strict design codes. Typical examples are the design of pressure boats, the design of speed reducers, the design of domes and towers, and the integration of optimization with finite element modeling and other structures. A very important but also very realistic question is how to select an algorithm for a given optimization problem in structural engineering. For unconventional algorithms, such as gradient-based algorithms, and simplex processes, we know what sort of problems they can normally solve. However, in the case of new algorithms, as in the case of most natural-inspired algorithms, we need to carry out comprehensive studies to verify and test their performance. Obviously, any detailed knowledge of a specific problem is often useful for the proper selection of the right and most successful optimization approaches. From the point of view of algorithm creation, how best to apply problem-specific knowledge is also an ongoing challenge. The no free lunch theorems for optimization given by D.H. Wolpert and W.G. Macready state that no algorithm is better than the other when the output metrics are averaged over all potential problems. Obviously, NFL keeps this area of research very involved and results in an annual improvement of existing methods and inception of new metaheuristics.

5. Conclusions

This chapter provides a state-of-the-art analysis of nature-inspired computing paradigms for optimal design problems in the field of structural engineering. Classical approaches tend to be stuck in local minima when dealing with complex real-world engineering optimization concerns. Using nature-inspired metaheuristics, the discovery of the entire search space is feasible due to the population involved and thus an optimal solution is reached.

References

[1] Z. Michalewicz, Genetic Algorithms + Data Structures = Evolution Programs, Springer-Verlag, Berlin, 1994.

[2] R.E. Griffith, R.A. Stewart, A nonlinear programming technique for the optimization of continuous processing systems, Manag. Sci. 7 (1961) 379–392.

[3] B.K. Kannan, S.N. Kramer, An augmented Lagrange multiplier based method for mixed integer discrete continuous optimization and its applications to mechanical design, J. Mech. Des. 116 (2) (1994) 405, https://doi.org/10.1115/1.2919393.

[4] J.S. Arora, Introduction to Optimum Design, McGraw-Hill, New York, 1989.

[5] Sandgren, E., Nonlinear integer and discrete programming in mechanical design, Proceedings.

[6] R.V. Rao, G.G. Waghmare, A new optimization algorithm for solving complex constrained design optimization problems, Eng. Optim. 49 (1) (2016) 60–83.

[7] K.S. Lee, Z.W. Geem, A new Meta -heuristic algorithm for continuous engineering optimization: harmony search theory and practice, Comput. Methods Appl. Mech. Eng. 194 (36–38) (2005) 3902–3933.

[8] J.H. Holland, Adaptation in Natural and Artificial Systems, University of Michigan Press, 1975.

[9] S. Kirkpatrick, C.D. Gelatt, M.P. Vecchi, Optimization by simulated annealing, Science 220 (4598) (1983) 671–680.

[10] D. Karaboga, B. Gorkemli, C. Ozturk, N. Karaboga, A comprehensive survey: artificial bee colony (ABC) algorithm and applications, Artif. Intell. Rev. 42 (2014) 21–57.

[11] G. Beni, J. Wang, Swarm intelligence in cellular robotic systems, in: NATO Advanced Workshop on Robots and Biological Systems, Il Ciocco, Tuscany, Italy, 1989.

[12] E. Bonabeau, M. Dorigo, G. Theraulaz, Swarm Intelligence: From Natural to Artificial Systems, Oxford University Press, 1999.

[13] G. Theraulaz, E. Bonabeau, A brief history of Stigmergy, Artif. Life 5 (1999) 97–116.

[14] V. Tereshko, A. Loengarov, Collective decision making in honey-bee foraging dynamics, Comput. Inf. Syst. 9 (3) (2005) 1–7.

[15] M. Dorigo, A. Colorni, V. Maniezzo, Positive feedback as a search strategy, Technical Report 91-016, Dipartimento di Elettronica, Politecnico di Milano, Milan, Italy, 1991.

[16] J. Kennedy, R. Eberhart, Particle swarm optimization, in: IEEE International Conference on Neural Networks, vol. 4, 1995, pp. 1942–1948.

[17] W.J. Teahan, Directions for bio-inspired artificial intelligence, J. Comput. Sci. Syst. Biol. 5 (2012) i–iii.

[18] S. Binitha, S.S. Sathya, A survey of bio inspired optimization algorithms, Int. J. Soft Comput. Eng. 2 (2) (2012).

[19] J.H. Holland, Genetic algorithms and the optimal allocation of trials, SIAM J. Comput. 2 (2) (1973) 88–105.

[20] J. Koza, R. Genetic, Programming: On the Programming of Computers by Means of Natural Selection, The MIT Press, Cambridge, MA, 1992.

[21] R. Storn, K. Price, Differential evolution—a simple and efficient heuristic for global optimization over continuous spaces, J. Glob. Optim. 11 (4) (1997) 341–359.

[22] Z.W. Geem, J.H. Kim, G.V. Loganathan, A new heuristic optimization algorithm: harmony search, SIMULATION 76 (2) (2001) 60–68.

[23] R.P. Feynman, Quantum mechanical computers, Found. Phys. 16 (6) (1986) 507–531.

[24] R.P. Feynman, Simulating physics with computers, Int. J. Theor. Phys. 21 (6–7) (1982) 467–488.

[25] Q. He, L. Wang, An effective co-evolutionary particle swarm optimization for constrained engineering design problems, Eng. Appl. Artif. Intel. 20 (2007) 89–99.

[26] P. Fourie, A. Groenwold, The particle swarm optimization in topology optimization, in: Fourth world congress of structural and multidisciplinary optimization, Paper no. 154, Dalian, China, 2001.

[27] G. Venter, J. Sobieszczanski-Sobieski, Multidisciplinary optimization of a transport aircraft wing using particle swarm optimization, Struct. Multidiscip. Optim. 26 (1–2) (2004) 121–131.

[28] E.R. Perez, K. Behdinan, Particle swarm optimization in structural design, in: F.T.S. Chan, M.K. Tiwari (Eds.), Swarm Intelligence, Focus on Ant and Particle Swarm Optimization, Itech Education and Publishing, Vienna, Austria, 2007, p. 532.

[29] C.V. Camp, B.J. Meyer, P.J. Palazolo, Particle Swarm optimization for the design of trusses, in: Structures 2004, ASCE, 2004, pp. 1–10.

[30] C.K. Dimou, V.K. Koumousis, Reliability-based optimal design of truss structures using particle swarm optimization, J. Comput. Civ. Eng. 32 (2) (2009) 100–109.

[31] T.J.M. McCarthy, S. McCluskey, A particle swarm optimization approach to reinforced concrete beam design according to AS 3600, in: Proceedings of the First International Conference on Soft Computing Technology in Civil Engineering, Stirlingshire, Scotland, 2009, pp. 1–14.

[32] B.A. Nedushan, H. Varaee, Minimum cost design of concrete slabs using particle swarm optimization with time varying acceleration coefficients, World Appl. Sci. J. 13 (12) (2011) 2484–2494.

[33] M. Khajehzadeh, M.R. Taha, A. Elshafie, M. Eslami, Modified particle swarm optimization for optimum design of spread footing and retaining wall, J. Zhejiang Univ. Sci. A 12 (6) (2011) 415–427.

[34] E. Dogan, M.P. Saka, Optimum design of unbraced steel frames to LRFD-AISC using particle swarm optimization, Adv. Eng. Softw. 46 (1) (2012) 27–34.

[35] F. Karpat, A virtual tool for minimum cost design of a wind turbine tower with ring stiffeners, Energies 6 (2013) 3822–3840.

[36] J.A. Bland, Optimal structural design by ant colony optimization, Eng. Optim. 33 (4) (2001) 425–443.

[37] Camp, B. Bichon, S. Stovall, Design of steel frames using ant colony optimization, J. Struct. Eng. 131 (3) (2005) 369–379.

[38] A. Kaveh, S. Talatahari, An improved ant colony optimization for design of planar steel frames, Eng. Struct. 32 (3) (2010) 864–873.

[39] M. Ghazavi, S.B. Bonab, Optimization of reinforced concrete retaining walls using ant colony method, ISGSR 2011 (2011) 297–305.

[40] A. Kaveh, M.S. Massoudi, Cost optimization of a composite floor system using ant colony system, IJST Trans. Civ. Eng. Shiraz Univ. 36 (C2) (2012) 139–148.

[41] P. Sharafi, M.N.S. Hadi, L.H. The, Optimum span's lengths of multi-span reinforced concrete beams under dynamic loading, in: Topics on Dynamics of Civil Structures: Conference Proceedings of the Society for Experimental Mechanics Series 2012, vol. 1, 2012, pp. 353–361.

[42] S. Talatahari, Determining the optimum section of tunnels using ant colony optimization, Math. Probl. Eng. 2013 (2013) 1–7.

[43] A.H. Gandomi, X. She-Yang, A.H. Alavi, Mixed variable structural optimization using firefly algorithm, Comput. Struct. 89 (23–24) (2011) 2325–2336.

[44] L.F.F. Miguel, L.F.F. Miguel, Novel metaheuristic algorithms applied to optimization of structures, WSEAS Trans. Appl. Theor. Mech. 7 (3) (2012) 210–220.

[45] I. Aydogdu, A. Akin, M.P. Saka, Discrete design optimization of space steel frames using the adaptive firefly algorithms, in: Proceedings of the Eleventh International Conference on Computational Structures Technology, Stirlingshire, U.K., Civil-Comp Press, Paper-73, 2012.

[46] M. Khajehzadeh, M.R. Taha, M. Eslami, A new hybrid firefly algorithm for foundation optimization, Natl. Acad. Sci. Lett. 36 (3) (2013) 279–288.

[47] O. Hasancebi, T. Teke, O. Pekcan, A bat-inspired algorithm for structural optimization, Comput. Struct. 128 (2013) 77–90.

[48] S. Gholizadeh, V. Aligholizadeh, Optimum design of reinforced concrete frames using bat meta-heuristic algorithm, Int. J. Optim. Civ. Eng. 3 (3) (2013) 483–497.

[49] Carbas, S. and Hasancebi, O. "Optimum design of steel space frames via bat-inspired algorithm," Proceedings of the 10th World Congress on Structural and Multidisciplinary Optimization, May 19–24, 2013, Orlando, Florida, USA.

[50] A. Kaveh, P. Zakian, Enhanced bat algorithm for optimal design of skeletal structures, Asian J. Civ. Eng. 15 (2) (2014) 179–212.

[51] H. Garg, Solving structural engineering design optimization problems using an artificial bee colony algorithm, J. Ind. Manag. Optim. 10 (3) (2014) 777–794.

[52] M. Sonmez, Artificial bee colony algorithm for optimization of truss structures, Appl. Soft Comput. 11 (2) (2011) 2406–2418.

[53] S. Talatahari, M. Nouri, F. Tadbiri, Optimization of skeletal structures using artificial bee Colony algorithm, Int. J. Optim. Civ. Eng. 2 (4) (2012) 557–571.

[54] M.M. Jahjouh, M.H. Arafa, M.A. Alqedra, Artificial bee Colony (ABC) algorithm in the design optimization of RC continuous beams, Struct. Multidiscip. Optim. 47 (6) (2013) 963–979.

[55] Carbas, S., Aydogdu, I. and Saka, M.P. "A comparative study of three meta-heuristics for the optimum design of engineering structures," Proceedings of the 10th World Congress on Structural and Multidisciplinary Optimization, May 19–24, 2013, Orlando, Florida, USA.

[56] F. Kang, J. Li, Z. Ma, An artificial bee Colony algorithm for locating the critical slip circle in slope stability analysis, Eng. Optim. 45 (2) (2013) 207–223.

[57] S. Mirjalili, S.M. Mirjalili, A. Lewis, Grey wolf optimizer, Adv. Eng. Softw. 69 (2014) 46–61.

[58] S. Mirjalili, Dragonfly algorithm: a new meta-heuristic optimization technique for solving single-objective, discrete, and multi-objective problems, Neural Comput. Applic. 27 (4) (2015) 1053–1073.

[59] S. Mirjalili, Moth-flame optimization algorithm: a novel nature-inspired heuristic paradigm, Knowl.-Based Syst. 89 (2015) 228–249.

[60] S. Mirjalili, A. Lewis, The whale optimization algorithm, Adv. Eng. Softw. 95 (2016) 51–67.

[61] S. Mirjalili, A.H. Gandomi, S.Z. Mirjalili, S. Saremi, H. Faris, S.H. Mirjalili, Salp swarm algorithm: a bio-inspired optimizer for engineering design problems, Adv. Eng. Softw. 114 (2017) 163–191.

[62] S. Saremi, S. Mirjalili, A. Lewis, Grasshopper optimization algorithm: theory and application, Adv. Eng. Softw. 105 (2017) 30–47.

[63] M. Agarwal, Optimal solution of structural engineering design problems using crow search algorithm, Int. J. Math. Eng. Manag. Sci. 4 (4) (2019) 968–981.

[64] S.F. Hwang, R.S. He, A hybrid real-parameter genetic algorithm for function optimization, Adv. Eng. Inform. 20 (2006) 7–21.

[65] S. Rajeev, C.S. Krishnamoorthy, Discrete optimization of structures using genetic algorithms, ASCE J. Struct. Eng. 118 (5) (1992) 1233–1250.

[66] J. Sakamoto, J. Oda, Technique for optimal layout design for truss structures using genetic algorithms, in: Collection of Technical Papers-AIAA/ASME Structures, Structural Dynamics and Material Conference, Publ. by AIAA Washington DC, USA, Pt.4, 4402-2408, 1993.

[67] H. Adeli, N.T. Cheng, Integrated genetic algorithm for optimization of space structures, J. Aerosp. Eng. 6 (4) (1993) 315–328.

[68] V.K. Koumousis, P.G. Georgiou, Genetic algorithms in discrete optimization of steel truss roofs, J. Comput. Civ. Eng. 8 (3) (1994) 309–325.

[69] M. Ohsaki, Genetic algorithms for topology optimization of trusses, Comput. Struct. 57 (2) (1995) 219–225.

[70] C.K. Soh, J. Yang, Fuzzy controlled genetic algorithm search for shape optimization, J. Comput. Civ. Eng. 10 (2) (1996) 143–150, https://doi.org/10.1061/(asce)0887-3801(1996)10:2(143).

[71] E. Mezura-Montes, C.A. Coello Coello, J. Velázquez-Reyes, L. Muñoz-Davila, Multiple trial vectors in differential evolution for engineering design, Eng. Optim. 39 (5) (2007) 567–589, https://doi.org/10.1080/03052150701364022.

[72] S. Botello, J.L. Marroquin, E. Onate, J. Van Horebeek, Solving structural optimization problems with genetic algorithms and simulated annealing, Int. J. Numer. Methods Eng. 45 (1999) 1069–1084.

[73] L.S. Coelho, Gaussian quantum-behaved particle swarm optimization approaches for constrained engineering design problems, Expert Syst. Appl. 37 (2010) 1676–1683. 26, No. 1–2, pp. 121–131, 2004.

A data-driven model for fire safety strategies assessment using artificial neural networks and genetic algorithms

Rachid Ouache, Amin Mohammadpour Shotorbani, Kasun Hewage, and Rehan Sadiq
School of Engineering, University of British Columbia, Okanagan Campus, Kelowna, BC, Canada

1. Introduction

The building industry has seen a tremendous development in the last few years around the world. From 2013 to 2018, Canada has recorded an average value of $7.5 B per month from building permits, in which the major value part is spent on residential buildings. This helped to build an average of 15,000 multiunit residential buildings (MURBs) between April and August in 2018; besides, 6000 detached houses were built per month nationwide. To maintain quality and sustainability of residential buildings, protection against fires is found to be one of the main challenges that are posing a substantial threat to public safety, property, and the environment. According to the National Fire Information Database (NFID) [1], Canada has recorded almost half-million building fires between 2005 and 2015, among which ~67% of the fires occurred in residential buildings; ~5% of these fires were recorded within just seven cities of BC province. Furthermore, 55% of these fires were found to be recorded in MURBs and 36% in single-detached houses. Consequently, ~15,000 victims and ~$7B of economic loss during the same period were reported in Canada. Moreover, ~ 1200 children were injured during the period between 2006 and 2013.

Fire risk assessment (FRA) is an essential tool to control the above-mentioned catastrophic consequences [2–4]. Investigating fire protection and intervention strategies [1, 5, 6], including initial fire detection, the actions taken, and the method of fire control and extinguishment, will be necessary for FRA. The initial fire detection includes different technical factors, such as smoke and heat alarms, heat detectors, and automatic sprinkler system. The actions taken involve fire department and automatic sprinkler systems, whereas the method of fire control encompasses handheld extinguisher, standpipe and hose systems, sprinkler system, and fire department intervention. Transmission of an alarm to the fire department takes several potential informing ways into consideration, including telegraph or telephone systems, radio systems, private fire alarm as a smart system, radio system, direct verbal report to a fire station, telephone tie-line to a fire department, siren, horn, or another alerting device. These fire safety strategies help to achieve a common objective in protecting people, properties, and the environment [1, 7].

An integrated framework for fire risk assessment to develop safety strategies is required for the investigation, prediction, and optimization for fire control and mitigating related impacts [8, 9]. No comprehensive model is found in the published literature, which reliably addresses the prediction of fire-related impacts and recommends optimal fire safety strategies related to the protection and intervention for MURBs. Several empirical methods are used for prediction, such as regression analysis and artificial neural networks (ANNs) [10].

ANN is a robust method for detecting complex nonlinear relationships. Several researchers are found to use ANN [11–17]. Pedroni et al. found that ANN is an effective method compared to quadratic response surfaces in estimating the failure probability of a thermal-hydraulic passive system [18]. In addition, ANN assists in addressing the related aleatory and epistemic uncertainties, which are the main challenges in fire safety assessment [19–21]. Izquierdo et al. also used ANN to reduce the inherent epistemic uncertainty in reliability analysis [13]. ANN-based models are common in risk and safety investigations. Santhosh et al. used ANN for safety assessment to enhance prediction [22]; Pliego et al. used ANN to develop an approach for false alarm detection and prioritization to increase the system reliability [23]. Jafari et al. developed a model using ANN for forest fire risk focusing on occurrence analysis [8]. Ding et al. determined the fire rating of buildings for fire risk assessment in high-rise buildings using ANN to improve decision-making for fire safety [24]. Zheng et al. used ANN to evaluate fire risk for a shopping center [25]. Li et al. found that ANN performs better than polynomial regression analysis [26]. Besides, Rotshtein et al. proposed a tool to solve the fault diagnosis problem using a genetic algorithm [27]. Tsoukalas and Fragiadakis used a genetic algorithm to enhance the prediction of occupational risk in the shipbuilding industry. Furthermore, Jahed et al. found that a hybrid genetic algorithm-ANN model gave better results for airblast prediction [28]. Therefore, ANN and genetic algorithms are found to be suitable to develop a model to predict and optimize the possible fire impacts, as numerous variables and predictors are involved; furthermore, the model will have an ability to incorporate possible interactions between fire safety strategies and fire impacts using multiple algorithms.

This study aims to develop a data-driven model to guide the selection of the best fire safety strategies by integrating ANN and genetic algorithms. Proposed model attempts to address the following critical questions to enhance the fire safety strategies in MURBs:

(i) What are the key potential strategies for fire protection and intervention for MURBs?
(ii) How to predict possible fire impacts effectively and efficiently?
(iii) How to select the optimal combination of predictors that minimize fire impacts?

2. Methodology

The proposed model, which addresses the above-mentioned questions, is presented in Fig. 1. The model development was based on three main steps: (i) Identify possible fire strategies in multiunit residential buildings; (ii) develop an ANN model to predict the possible fire impacts based on the available safety strategies in MURBs, and (iii) use a genetic algorithm to minimize the fire impacts. The developed model was demonstrated through a case study of British Columbia based on the data of fire incidents

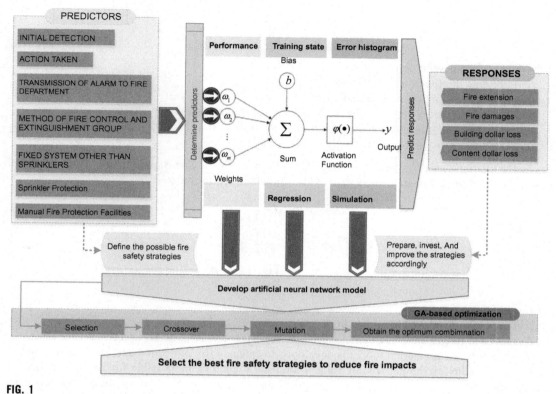

FIG. 1

Process of the developed model for fire strategies assessment.

collected for MURBs. In this study, safety strategies refer to all possible fire protection and intervention techniques to help reduce fire impacts in MURBs. Safety strategies take into consideration both protection and intervention safeguards to ensure that all aspects of fire safety are fully integrated. The details of the developed model are presented in the following subsections.

2.1 Development of ANN-based prediction model

Artificial neural network (ANN) is a common machine learning technique that was inspired by the principle of biological neural networks [13], where a collection of connected artificial neurons model the neurons in a brain. Therefore, ANN is considered to be an essential component of artificial intelligence to simulate the functioning of a human brain. Handling a large amount of dataset is an important aspect of ANN. Besides, ANN is capable of modeling complex nonlinear relationships among predictors and responses, detecting all possible interactions [11, 29]. A one-layer perceptron ANN can be described as:

$$y = f(\varphi) = f\left(\sum_{i=1}^{m} (w_i a_i) + b \right)$$

(1)

$$\varphi = W^T A + B \tag{2}$$

where

y refers to the neuron output;

$f(\varphi)$ presents the function of the summation output.

a_i and w_i refer to inputs and weights, respectively.

b refers to bias that is added to the weighted sum of the inputs to adjust the output. whereas, W^T represents the transpose of weight vectors, where $W = [w_1, w_2, w_3, \ldots, w_m]$ and A represents input vectors; $A = [a_1, a_2, a_3, \ldots, a_m]$.

Several activation functions have been used in ANN layers, including *Sigmoid*, *Tangent Hyperbolic* (*Tanh*), and *Rectified Linear Unit* (RELU) [11, 30], which are formulated as

$$Sigmoid : f(x) = \frac{1}{1 + e^{-x}} \tag{3}$$

$$Tanh : f(x) = \frac{2}{1 + e^{-2x}} - 1 \tag{4}$$

$$RELU : f(x) = \begin{cases} 0 & \text{for } x < 0 \\ x & \text{for } x \geq 0 \end{cases} \tag{5}$$

where

$f(x)$ in *Sigmoid* and *RELU* ranges from 0 to 1 and

$f(x)$ in *Tanh* ranges from -1 to 1.

The ANN-based prediction model is developed to enhance fire protection and intervention strategies. Seven predictors summarized in Table 1 are used to predict the possible fire impacts. The predictors are investigated from real fire scenarios using the National Fire Information Database. The factors of the predictors were coded according to the classifications. Initial detection represents the possible used means to detect a fire incident. The "action taken" presents the action that is conducted to combat the fire. The predictor of the method of fire control and extinguishment group classifies the

Table 1 Details of the seven predictors, safety strategies.	
Predictors	**Code**
(1) Initial detection	
Smoke alarm device	1
Smoke detector device	2
Heat alarm device	3
Heat detector device	4
(2) Action taken	
Extinguished by occupant	1
Burned out - no extinguishment attempted	2
Extinguished by fire department	3
Extinguished by an automatic system	4

Table 1 Details of the seven predictors, safety strategies—cont'd

Predictors	Code
(3) Method of fire control and extinguishment group	
Handheld extinguisher	1
Standpipe & hose systems (building)	2
Makeshift firefighting aids	3
Fire department - water	4
Fire department – other than water	5
Sprinkler system	6
Fixed system other than sprinklers	7
(4) Transmission of alarm to fire department	
Coded signal municipal fire alarm system (included are telegraph or telephone systems, radio systems, and auxiliary connection to them)	1
Private fire alarm system (included are signals received from central stations and remote stations)	2
Radio	3
Direct verbal report to a fire station	4
(5) Manual fire protection facilities	
Extinguishers and standpipe system	1
Extinguishers	2
Standpipe system	3
No manual fire protection	4
(6) Sprinkler protection	
Complete sprinkler protection - supervised or watchman service	1
Complete sprinkler protection - alarm to fire department	2
Complete sprinkler protection - unsupervised, local alarms only	3
Partial sprinkler protection - supervised or watchman service	4
Partial sprinkler protection - alarm to fire department	5
Partial sprinkler protection - unsupervised, local alarms only	6
(7) Fixed system other than sprinklers	
Supervised or watchman service	1
Alarm to fire departments	2
Unsupervised, local alarms only	3
No fixed system	4
Dry chemical system	5

specifically used method to control and extinguish the fire. Manual fire protection facilities indicate the hand fire extinguishers as well as the standpipe and hose systems. The sprinkler protection system is used to present several cases, including the coverage of sprinkler protection, complete where the system is installed throughout the building, with the possible enhancement, such as an alarm to the fire department. Conformance with NFPA 13 considers a structure to be fully protected by a sprinkler system. Besides, the building could be supported with several facilities, including standard watchman service, and transmission to fire alarm headquarters. A fixed system other than sprinklers presents any other systems besides sprinkler systems, such as dry chemical systems. Correlation analysis is performed between the predictors and the responses.

Regarding the responses, fire extension (FE) and fire damages (FD) are classified in seven categories to present fire impacts for both extension and damages, respectively (Table 2). This table presents five levels for building in terms of "dollar loss" and the "content dollar loss" based on the recorded dollar loss from the previous fire incidents. The levels of building and content dollar losses include *very high* (VH = 5), *high* (H = 4), *medium* (M = 3), *low* (L = 2), and *very low* (VL = 1) for percentages [(max) | average (max, average) | average | average (average, min)| average (average (average, min), min)], respectively.

Three algorithms are used in the development of ANN model to enhance prediction accuracy, including Levenberg-Marquardt (LM), scaled conjugate gradient (SCG), and Bayesian regularization (BR) backpropagation algorithms [31]. The percentages 70%, 15%, and 15% of the data were used for training, validation, and testing, respectively. Mean squared error (MSE) and correlation coefficient (R) are used to determine the performance of the ANN model. MSE measures the average squared error between the estimated values and the actual target values. R is used as a numerical measure of some type of correlation. The strength of the model is represented as very weak *(VW)*, weak *(W)*, moderately strong *(MS)*, strong *(S)*, very strong *(VS)*, or perfect *(P)* that corresponds to the R-values of <0.2, <0.4, <0.6, <0.8, <1, or 1, respectively [32]. A weight-based code for MATLAB function is produced as a deployable solution of the trained ANN to generate results and solve similar problems.

Table 2 Details of the fire impact responses.

Fire damages (FD)		Fire extension (FE)		Dollar loss		
1	Confined to part of room/area of origin	1	Confined to object of origin	Levels	BDL	CDL
2	Confined to a room of origin	2	Confined to part of room/area of origin	VL	$ 5000.00	$ 10,000.00
3	Confined to the floor level of origin	3	Confined to room of origin	L	$ 50,049.94	$ 22,625.84
4	Confined to the building of origin	4	Confined to floor level of origin	M	$ 95,099.87	$ 35,251.69
5	Extended beyond the building of origin	5	Confined to building of origin	H	$ 20,047,549.94	$ 5,017,625.84
6	Confined to roof	6	Extended beyond building of origin	VH	$ 40,000,000.00	$ 10,000,000.00
7	Not applicable (includes vehicle, outside area)	7	Confined to roof	Dollar loss levels, very high (VH), high (H), medium (M), low (L), and very low (VL), are determined based on recorded values of fire incidents for max value (max) of dollar loss for fire incidents, average (max, average), average, average (average, min), and average (average (average, min), min), respectively.		

The developed MATLAB code for ANN modeling after importing the data including the model *Inputs* and *Targets* is presented as follows:

```
%import Inputs with size: number of samples * number of variables
%import Targets with size: number of samples * number of output variables
global net %net will be used for optimization via GA
net = fitnet([50],'trainbr');
net = train(net,Inputs,Targets);
output = net(Inputs);
perf_train = perform(net,output,Targets);
```

The ANN model is developed based on the function fitting neural network (i.e., fitnet) with one hidden layer with 50 neurons. The ANN model is trained using the Levenberg-Marquardt optimization back-propagation algorithm (i.e., 'trainbr'). Other training algorithms can be 'traingd', 'trainbr', 'traingdm', 'traingdx', and 'traincgp', of which we obtained the best performance with the 'trainbr'. The estimation performance of the ANN model is calculated using the perform function. The code uses the default training parameters of the 'trainbr' training function, which are shown in Table 3.

Different training methods (including trainlm, traingdx, traincgp, trainbr) and the number of layers (1–3 layers) were applied, and the 1-layer ANN with the trainlm training function was selected, as it showed the best performance (i.e., 0.83) with the lowest estimation as error(1) = 0.1684 error(2) = 0.1645 error(3) = 0.1504. The One Hot Key Encoder was not used, as it did not improve the performance of the ANN.

2.2 Optimization using multiobjective-based genetic algorithms

The multiobjective-based genetic algorithm is an exceptionally effective technique in providing a search strategy, generating possible solutions, and optimizing multidimensional problems [33, 34]. The genetic algorithm is considered to have three fundamentals: (i) ability to define fitness criterion; (ii) ability to articulate the solution as a chromosome, generally as an array of bits; and finally (iii) ability to imitate sexual reproduction, crossover, and mutation; crossover is a process of exchanging bits between the solutions. The crossover of two-parent strings produces new solutions, whereas

Table 3 Training parameters of the `trainbr` training function.

Training parameters	net.trainParam	Value
Maximum number of epochs	.epochs	1000
mu: Initial/maximum	.mu/.mu_max	0.001/1e10
mu Increase/decrease factor	.mu_inc/.mu_dec	10/0.1
Performance goal	.goal	0
Minimum performance gradient	.min_grad	1e−7
Maximum number of validation failures	.max_fail	6

mutation is generating new solutions by flipping some bits of a string. An objective function (Obj) in a genetic algorithm, as presented in Eq. 6, describes the objective of the optimization [35].

$$Obj = \frac{\sum_{i=1}^{P} (d_i(p_i) \cdot weight_i)}{\sum_{i=1}^{P} weight_i} \tag{6}$$

where the formula is normalized, by dividing with the sum of all the weights; $weight_i$ corresponds to the relative importance of each property i; d_i represents the desirability as a function that should be low in this case as minimizing the outcome of risk.

The developed code for multiobjective-based GA optimization is presented as follows:

```
%X = ga(FITNESSFCN,NVARS,A,b,Aeq,beq,lb,ub,NONLCON)
ObjectiveFunction= @(x)[obj1(x) obj2(x) obj3(x)];
nvars = 7; % Number of variables
A1=[];
b1=[];
Aeq1=[];
beq1=[];
LB1 = [1 1 1 1 1 1 1]; % Lower bound
UB1 = [4 4 4 7 5 6 5]; % Upper bound
ConstraintFunction=[];
opts=optimoptions(@gamultiobj,'MaxGenerations', 300,'MaxStallGenerations',
100);
%EVALUATION
[bestX,bestfval]=gamultiobj(ObjectiveFunction,nvars,A1,b1,Aeq1,beq1,LB1,UB1,
ConstraintFunction,opts)
```

where obj1(x) obj2(x) obj3(x) are separate functions defined as

function y=obj1(x)	function y=obj2(x)	function y=obj3(x)
global net	global net	global net
y1=net(x');	y1=net(x');	y1=net(x');
y=round(y1(1,:));	y=round(y1(2,:));	y=round(y1(3,:));
end	end	end

3. Results and discussions

3.1 Investigation of fire safety predictors

The fire safety strategies for almost 1000 fire incidents are investigated in the BC province of Canada. Fig. 2 shows three of the investigated safety strategies for the first 25 fire incidents. In the initial detection strategies, it is found that 67% of the fire incidents were detected visually. It is followed by a smoke alarm device and smoke detector device with 15.6% and 13.9% of the fire incidents, respectively. Regarding the transmission of alarm to fire department, 57.8% of the fires had telephone tie-line to fire department; the coded signal municipal fire alarm system, including telephone and radio systems, is associated with 38.8%, as the second high, of the recorded fires in MURBs. Concerning

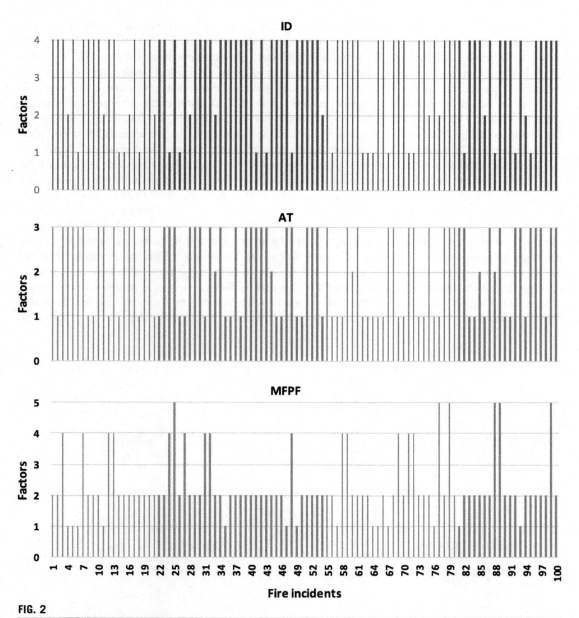

FIG. 2

The identified safety strategy factors.

the taken actions, it is found that around 45% of the fire incidents were extinguished by the fire department. It is followed by fires extinguished by the occupants, which were 41.8%. Approximately 10% of the fire incidents could not be extinguished. Automatic systems extinguished just 3.1% of the occurred fires.

The most used methods for fire control and extinguishment are as follows: fire department using water – 30.8%, makeshift firefighting aids – ~30%, and handheld equipment – 19.8% of the fires extinguished. Regarding the manual fire protection facilities, extinguishers were used in 60.7% of the cases. Extinguishers and standpipe were used together in 19.2% of the incidents, whereas no manual fire protection was used for 12.6% of the fire incidents. Regarding the sprinkler protection, it is found that 73.7% of the fire incidents had no sprinkler protection and 12.2% of the fires had no applicability of the sprinkler system. Finally, regarding the fixed systems other than sprinklers, it is found that 75.6% of the fire incidents had no fixed system, whereas in 9.3% of the cases alarms to fire departments were fixed.

A contour plot is shown in Fig. 3 to investigate the relationship between the content dollar loss and two predictors. This shows that having a sprinkler system with a smoke detector device led to having a *high level* of content dollar loss, whereas having a sprinkler system or fire department intervention with almost all initial detection techniques caused a *medium level* of content dollar loss. This also shows that having partial sprinkler protection with supervised or watchman service and fire department intervention caused a content dollar loss to reach the *high* and *very high* levels. It can also be seen that in case of having a partial sprinkler system or not having it at all with the intervention of the fire department gives a wide range of having a *medium level* of content dollar loss. Regarding the fire safety strategies of the initial detection and transmission of alarm to the fire department, it can be seen that having a smoke detector device or automatic sprinkler system with a private fire alarm system or radio, respectively, caused a very high level of content dollar loss. Based on these strategies, it can be seen that there is a higher potential of a high level of content dollar loss. Moreover, having a fire department or sprinkler

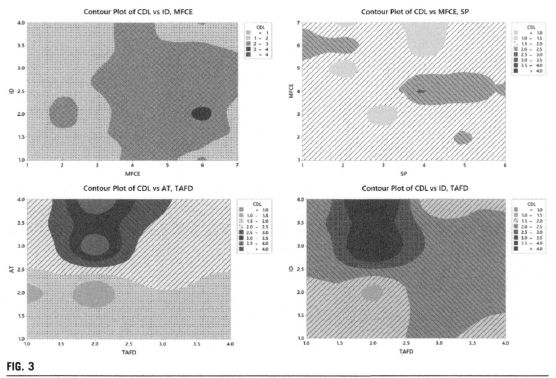

FIG. 3

A contour plot for content dollar loss.

system as the possible taken actions with a private fire alarm system or radio shows a range of *high* and *very high levels* of content dollar loss.

3.2 Artificial neural network and genetic algorithm

The results of the developed ANN model for the prediction of potential fire impacts are presented in this section. The Bayesian regularization algorithm is found to be preferred based on the high value of the correlation coefficient. Fig. 4 shows the results of the Bayesian regularization algorithm with 1000 iterations. The Bayesian regularization algorithm is selected for predicting fire impact's accuracy. It is found that the best R-value for the Bayesian regularization algorithm is 0.68 at an epoch of 189 for training, whereas the total R-value is 0.67. The error histogram with 20 bins shows that most of the datasets have a low error of 0.19.

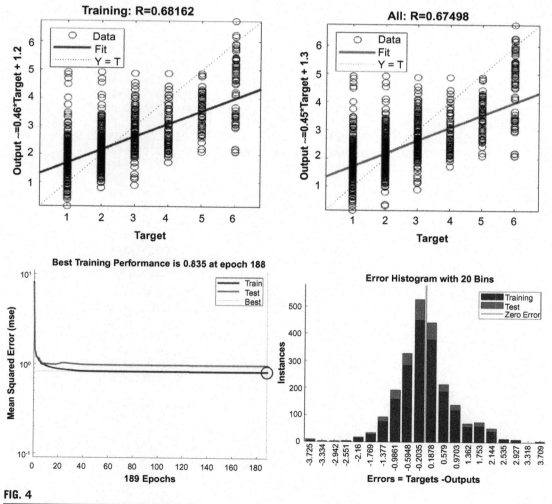

FIG. 4

Results of Bayesian regularization algorithm.

A MATLAB function [36, 37] is generated to produce results and solve similar problems, as follows:

```
function [Y,Xf,Af] = myNeuralNetworkFunction(X,~,~)
% [Y] = myNeuralNetworkFunction(X,~,~) takes these arguments:
%   X = 1xTS cell, 1 inputs over TS timesteps
%   Each X{1,ts} = 7xQ matrix, input #1 at timestep ts.
% and returns:
%   Y = 1xTS cell of 1 outputs over TS timesteps.
%   Each Y{1,ts} = 3xQ matrix, output #1 at timestep ts.
% where Q is number of samples (or series) and TS is the number of timesteps.
% ===== NEURAL NETWORK CONSTANTS =====
% Input 1
x1_step1.xoffset = [1;1;1;1;1;1;1];
x1_step1.gain    = [0.666666666666667;0.666666666666667;0.666666666666667;
0.333333333333333;0.5;0.4;0.5];
x1_step1.ymin = -1;

% Layer 1
b1=[-1.1975165116001682541;-0.41197963888286764922;-0.63364161285769471377;
0.21954310609185728742;0.06683555270761977473737;1.0506584618966829936;
0.39777266735658933783;0.22882403856442581902;-1.051888176844380185;-
2.3553780566168160959];
IW1_1=[-1.153133840723160608-0.46310639928762220574 0.26295388174075123855 -
0.46389740528460254865 -0.32592936354950879929 1.9009495249305254916 -
0.2670744408644937784;-0.1154037636507263126 0.50553796352779578616 -
0.42126125069428954628 -1.6381959117696969219 0.55901819952367592936
0.66974330430725015351 -0.6984588153370985264;-0.047286477688142883324 -
0.83208943904325483043 0.33657415529274281596 -0.31148647069490986716 -
0.69319952335929024834 0.0042723452226380732172
0.9930885651314502737378;0.19522854492884431088 1.2073781108664654038 -
1.708234337295749139 0.20437119123147751143 0.85983606982382554396
0.076549393205337407098 -1.1984982970384869816;-0.6461873179461808947 -
0.51169572506351612695 -0.2602549216948537504 -0.1361385448493377115 -
1.2913983668445510045 -0.9817470468874269734 0.12101275482321549593;-
0.32078635722150278253 -0.46093541416265298993 0.3395531977876889429 -
1.1347245620531358767 0.18698380109156323425 -1.1759318743096531801
0.74536271753509963922;0.12482890806677164608 0.67758363459714288091
1.04509890362166602 -1.8462361258604673697 -0.4663467447694586987
0.21217416353718188127 -0.8249381369036326785;-0.17541709185117945746 -
1.2463863011746472154 -0.22410266777173037944 -1.1278240370264047687
0.71294154676175114371 -0.92057513422764636335
1.2999213976690158212;0.19525568827216618906 0.4194201687405962331
0.57447045668311913502 -0.3679101671050425959 0.13681544455876409883
0.73559737623347820623 1.3143819041412996285;0.24562634084493742415
0.2561318757699196369 -0.15285786780334620349 -0.136794184952595127
0.71748266836889296183 0.81338773332022695772 1.7809085341812433967]];
```

```
% Layer 2
b2 = [-0.047043086757106292173;0.064648558395429808754;-
0.66789645929910101962];
LW2_1 = [0.42086049649803436434 -0.74597945567890378005 1.4778717435327668461
0.90276848866645320602 -0.74924470410559607103 0.82849426531368064452
0.49809969037650814183 -0.88715195024917681277 -0.75894882971367139124
1.1362909498440387779;0.42612898192499731875 -0.86512231196773492492
1.3885590477381668517 0.87646698385232657547 -0.72894520528664263903
0.79042934701976541589 0.62007336385522071609 -0.83693471912626249409 -
0.81552772739941670199 1.2377570403434472457;0.18038413535102326701 -
0.40680408941307483195 0.48251207980917054652 0.27678937595780844783 -
0.56982782018029110027 0.55085787735477442784 0.269609584626872123 -
0.39067071859942609224 -0.33756313517992625473 -0.0086168823718965614766];

% Output 1
y1_step1.ymin = -1;
y1_step1.gain = [0.4;0.4;0.666666666666667];
y1_step1.xoffset = [1;1;1];

% ===== SIMULATION ========
% Format Input Arguments
isCellX = iscell(X);
if ~isCellX
    X = {X};
end
% Dimensions
TS = size(X,2); % timesteps
if ~isempty(X)
    Q = size(X{1},2); % samples/series
else
    Q = 0;
end
% Allocate Outputs
Y = cell(1,TS);

% Time loop
for ts=1:TS

    % Input 1
    Xp1 = mapminmax_apply(X{1,ts},x1_step1);

    % Layer 1
    a1 = tansig_apply(repmat(b1,1,Q) + IW1_1*Xp1);

    % Layer 2
    a2 = repmat(b2,1,Q) + LW2_1*a1;

    % Output 1
    Y{1,ts} = mapminmax_reverse(a2,y1_step1);
end
```

```
% Final Delay States
Xf = cell(1,0);
Af = cell(2,0);
% Format Output Arguments
if ~isCellX
    Y = cell2mat(Y);
end
end


% ===== MODULE FUNCTIONS ========
% Map Minimum and Maximum Input Processing Function
function y = mapminmax_apply(x,settings)
y = bsxfun(@minus,x,settings.xoffset);
y = bsxfun(@times,y,settings.gain);
y = bsxfun(@plus,y,settings.ymin);
end

% Sigmoid Symmetric Transfer Function
function a = tansig_apply(n,~)
a = 2./ (1 + exp(-2*n)) - 1;
end

% Map Minimum and Maximum Output Reverse-Processing Function
function x = mapminmax_reverse(y,settings)
x = bsxfun(@minus,y,settings.ymin);
x = bsxfun(@rdivide,x,settings.gain);
x = bsxfun(@plus,x,settings.xoffset);
end
```

A genetic algorithm optimization is used to identify the optimal safety strategies (OSS) that jointly optimize a set of responses in reducing fire impacts. Fig. 5 shows the first 10 best scenarios in controlling fire impacts. The first optimal set of the predictors involves all the first factors of the predictors (code = 1), including the smoke alarm device, fire extinguished by the occupant, handheld extinguisher, extinguishers, and stand-pipe system, complete sprinkler protection – supervised or watchman service, fixed system other than sprinkler – supervised or watchman service, and coded signal municipal fire alarm system (included are the telegraph or telephone systems, radio systems, and the auxiliary connection to them).

Regarding the first research question, investigation of real fire incidents from the NFID discovered seven predictors that involve several factors as the key potential strategies for fire protection and intervention for MURBs.

The strategies cover initial detection, action taken, method of fire control and extinguishment group, manual fire protection facilities, sprinkler protection, fixed system other than sprinklers, and transmission of alarm to fire department. The discovered results for the most used fire safety strategies in MURBs support the claim of identifying trends in fire incidents that help to identify target hazards and enhance fire and life safety education programs [38, 39]. Concerning the second research question in predicting possible fire impacts, the ANN model is developed with a strong ability to predict the possible fire impacts from different perspectives, including fire damages, fire extension, content dollar loss, and content

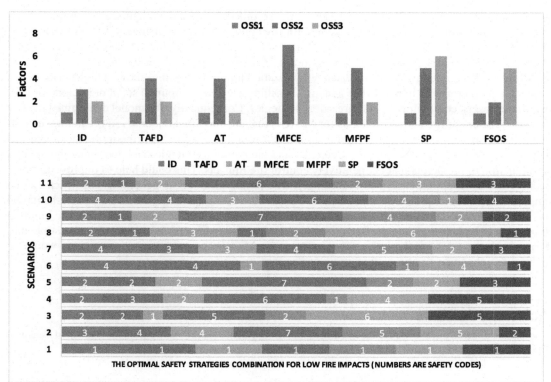

Note: OSS: optimal safety strategies, **AT**: ACTION TAKEN, **MFCE**: METHOD OF FIRE CONTROL AND EXTINGUISHMENT GROUP, **TAFD**: TRANSMISSION OF ALARM TO FIRE DEPARTMENT, **MFPF**: MANUAL FIRE PROTECTION FACILITIES, **SP**: SPRINKLER PROTECTION, **FSOS**: FIXED SYSTEM OTHER THAN SPRINKLERS

FIG. 5

Results of genetic algorithm-based optimization.

dollar loss. The optimal combination of safety strategies that minimize fire impacts is selected using a genetic algorithm. Selecting these strategies helps the decision-makers to enforce and use appropriate fire safety strategies for controlling fire impacts better. This supports the claim of Cowlard et al. [40] that the decision-makers should consider all potential strategies for enhancing fire protection.

4. Conclusions

This study developed a model for fire protection and optimization of protection and intervention strategies in MURBs to help investigate, predict, and optimize fire safety strategies. The developed model was applied to a case study in British Columbia, Canada. Fire safety strategies for protection and intervention are categorized by seven predictors. The most used fire safety strategies are identified, where more than 65% of the fire incidents were detected visually. Concerning transmission of alarm to the fire department, it is found that ~58% of the fires had telephone tie-line to the fire department. The investigation found that almost 45% of the fires were extinguished by the fire department as the taken actions to extinguish the fire. It is found that ~31% of the recorded fires were extinguished with the fire department using water as the most used method for fire control and extinguishment. Extinguishers were found to be used for ~61% of the cases as the manual fire protection facilities. It is found that ~74% of the fires had no sprinkler; besides, it is found that ~76% of the fire incidents had no system fixed. The developed ANN model using the Bayesian regularization training algorithm shows a high performance of 0.83 in predicting fire impacts. The genetic algorithm selected the optimal set of predictors for very low fire impacts, combining several fire safety strategies. Consequently, the model determined the key potential factors of fire safety strategies for MURBs that are classified under seven predictors, including manual fire protection facilities, sprinkler protection, and action taken. Furthermore, the model was able to predict fire impacts using fire protection and intervention strategies and determine the optimal combination of predictors that cooperatively control fire impacts. This could help to improve fire protection and intervention strategies accordingly. The proposed model is generalizable, which can be implemented in other provinces of Canada and other countries around the world. However, the model is limited to MURBs; therefore, the related protection and intervention strategies to specific building types should be investigated for effective results. Future research on the ignition and combustible materials with the most appropriate safety strategies for MURBs using artificial intelligence would be helpful in enhancing fire protection and intervention.

Acknowledgments

The authors gratefully acknowledge the funding support from NSERC, data obtained from the Council of Canadian Fire Marshals and Fire Commissioners, and the Canadian Association of Fire Chiefs.

References

[1] Public Safety Canada, National Fire Information Database (NFID), 2017.
[2] K. Tillander, Utilisation of Statistics to Assess Fire Risks in Buildings, VTT Publ, 2004, pp. 3–224.
[3] C. Guanquan, W. Jinhui, Study on probability distribution of fire scenarios in risk assessment to emergency evacuation, Reliab. Eng. Syst. Saf. 99 (2012) 24–32, https://doi.org/10.1016/j.ress.2011.10.014.
[4] K. Frank, M. Spearpoint, N. Challands, Uncertainty in estimating the fire control effectiveness of sprinklers from New Zealand fire incident reports, Fire Technol. 50 (2014) 611–632, https://doi.org/10.1007/s10694-012-0297-2.
[5] M. Vito, et al., Fire Service Features of Buildings and Fire Protection Systems, Occupational Safety and Health Administration, 2015.
[6] D. Barber, R. Gerard, Summary of the fire protection foundation report—fire safety challenges of tall wood buildings, Fire Sci. Rev. 4 (2015) 5, https://doi.org/10.1186/s40038-015-0009-3.
[7] D.M.Ã. Hanea, H.M. Jagtman, L.L.M.M. Van Alphen, B.J.M. Ale, Quantitative and qualitative analysis of the expert and non-expert opinion in fire risk in buildings, Reliab. Eng. Syst. Saf. 95 (2010) 729–741, https://doi.org/10.1016/j.ress.2010.02.011.
[8] Y. Jafari Goldarag, A. Mohammadzadeh, A.S. Ardakani, Fire risk assessment using neural network and logistic regression, J. Indian Soc. Remote Sens. 44 (2016) 885–894, https://doi.org/10.1007/s12524-016-0557-6.
[9] X. Sun, M. Luo, Fire risk assessment for super high-rise buildings, Procedia Eng. 71 (2014) 492–501, https://doi.org/10.1016/j.proeng.2014.04.071.

[10] M. Frandes, B. Timar, D. Lungeanu, A risk based neural network approach for predictive modeling of blood glucose dynamics, Stud. Health Technol. Inform. 228 (2017) 577–581, https://doi.org/10.3233/978-1-61499-678-1-577.

[11] R.C. Deo, M. Şahin, Ş. Mehmet, M. Şahin, Application of the artificial neural network model for prediction of monthly standardized precipitation and evapotranspiration index using hydrometeorological parameters and climate indices in eastern Australia, Atmos. Res. 161–162 (2015) 65–81, https://doi.org/10.1016/j.atmosres.2015.03.018.

[12] G. Bosque, I. del Campo, J. Echanobe, Fuzzy systems, neural networks and neuro-fuzzy systems: a vision on their hardware implementation and platforms over two decades, Eng. Appl. Artif. Intel. 32 (2014) 283–331,- https://doi.org/10.1016/j.engappai.2014.02.008.

[13] J. Izquierdo, A. Crespo Márquez, J. Uribetxebarria, Dynamic artificial neural network-based reliability considering operational context of assets, Reliab. Eng. Syst. Saf. 188 (2019) 483–493, https://doi.org/10.1016/j.ress.2019.03.054.

[14] O. Kocadağlı, A novel hybrid learning algorithm for full Bayesian approach of artificial neural networks, Appl. Soft Comput. 35 (2015) 52–65, https://doi.org/10.1016/j.asoc.2015.06.003.

[15] M. De Beule, E. Maes, O. De Winter, W. Vanlaere, R. Van Impe, Artificial neural networks and risk stratification: a promising combination, Math. Comput. Model. 46 (2007) 88–94, https://doi.org/10.1016/j.mcm.2006.12.024.

[16] G. Falavigna, G. Costantino, R. Furlan, J.V. Quinn, A. Ungar, R. Ippoliti, Artificial neural networks and risk stratification in emergency departments, Intern. Emerg. Med. 14 (2019) 291–299, https://doi.org/10.1007/s11739-018-1971-2.

[17] V. Karri, T. Ho, O. Madsen, Artificial neural networks and neuro-fuzzy inference systems as virtual sensors for hydrogen safety prediction, Int. J. Hydrogen Energy 33 (2008) 2857–2867, https://doi.org/10.1016/j.ijhydene.2008.02.039.

[18] N. Pedroni, E. Zio, G.E. Apostolakis, Comparison of bootstrapped artificial neural networks and quadratic response surfaces for the estimation of the functional failure probability of a thermal-hydraulic passive system, Reliab. Eng. Syst. Saf. 95 (2010) 386–395, https://doi.org/10.1016/j.ress.2009.11.009.

[19] Y. Dong, D.M. Frangopol, Probabilistic ship collision risk and sustainability assessment considering risk attitudes, Struct. Saf. 53 (2015) 75–84, https://doi.org/10.1016/j.strusafe.2014.10.004.

[20] T. Aven, S. Guikema, Whose uncertainty assessments (probability distributions) does a risk assessment report: the analysts or the experts? Reliab. Eng. Syst. Saf. 96 (2011) 1257–1262, https://doi.org/10.1016/j.ress.2011.05.001.

[21] J. Gehandler, H. Ingason, A. Lönnermark, H. Frantzich, M. Strömgren, Performance-based design of road tunnel fire safety: proposal of new Swedish framework, Case Stud. Fire Saf. 1 (2014) 18–28, https://doi.org/10.1016/j.csfs.2014.01.002.

[22] T.V. Santhosh, V. Gopika, A.K. Ghosh, B.G. Fernandes, An approach for reliability prediction of instrumentation & control cables by artificial neural networks and Weibull theory for probabilistic safety assessment of NPPs, Reliab. Eng. Syst. Saf. 170 (2018) 31–44, https://doi.org/10.1016/j.ress.2017.10.010.

[23] A. Pliego Marugán, A.M. Peco Chacón, F.P. García Márquez, Reliability analysis of detecting false alarms that employ neural networks: a real case study on wind turbines, Reliab. Eng. Syst. Saf. 191 (2019) 106574, https://doi.org/10.1016/j.ress.2019.106574.

[24] Y. Ding, F. Weng, J. Yu, Applying BP neural network in high-rising buildings fire risk assessment, in: 2011 3rd Int. Conf. Adv. Comput. Control. ICACC 2011, 2011, pp. 265–268, https://doi.org/10.1109/ICACC.2011.6016411.

[25] X. Zheng, P. Hu, J. Gao, Application of BP neural network in fire risk assessment of comprehensive shopping mall, in: Proc. 2019 Int. Conf. Intell. Comput. Autom. Syst. ICICAS 2019, 2019, pp. 416–420, https://doi.org/10.1109/ICICAS48597.2019.00093.

[26] L.M. Li, W.G. Song, J. Ma, K. Satoh, Artificial neural network approach for modeling the impact of population density and weather parameters on forest fire risk, Int. J. Wildland Fire 18 (2009) 640–647, https://doi.org/10.1071/WF07136.

[27] A.P. Rotshtein, M. Posner, H.B. Rakytyanska, Cause and effect analysis by fuzzy relational equations and a genetic algorithm, Reliab. Eng. Syst. Saf. 91 (2006) 1095–1101, https://doi.org/10.1016/j.ress.2005.11.041.

[28] D. Jahed, A. Mahdi, H. Amir, Airblast prediction through a hybrid genetic algorithm-ANN model, Neural Comput. Applic. 29 (2018) 619–629, https://doi.org/10.1007/s00521-016-2598-8.

[29] S.A. Adedigba, F. Khan, M. Yang, Dynamic failure analysis of process systems using neural networks, Process. Saf. Environ. Prot. 111 (2017) 529–543, https://doi.org/10.1016/j.psep.2017.08.005.

[30] M.Q. Raza, A. Khosravi, A review on artificial intelligence based load demand forecasting techniques for smart grid and buildings, Renew. Sustain. Energy Rev. 50 (2015) 1352–1372, https://doi.org/10.1016/j.rser.2015.04.065.

[31] MathWorks, Levenberg-Marquardt Backpropagation—MATLAB Trainlm, 2006. https://www.mathworks.com/help/deeplearning/ref/trainlm.html;jsessionid=519e8a3896bcf581a3a1d15c37e9. (Accessed March 25, 2020).

[32] M. Helmer, S. Warrington, J. Lisa, A. Howell, B. Rosand, Reliable Estimation of Canonical Correlation Analysis (CCA) and Partial Least Squares (PLS) with Application to Brain-Behavior Associations, bioRxiv, 2020. https://doi.org/10.1101/2020.08.25.265546.

[33] R. Mena, M. Hennebel, Y.-F. Li, C. Ruiz, E. Zio, A risk-based simulation and multi-objective optimization framework for the integration of distributed renewable generation and storage, Renew. Sustain. Energy Rev. 37 (2014) 778–793, https://doi.org/10.1016/j.rser.2014.05.046.

[34] V.D. Tsoukalas, N.G. Fragiadakis, Prediction of occupational risk in the shipbuilding industry using multivariable linear regression and genetic algorithm analysis, Saf. Sci. 83 (2016) 12–22, https://doi.org/10.1016/j.ssci.2015.11.010.

[35] J. Carr, An Introduction to Genetic Algorithms, Semantic Scholar, 2014.

[36] R. Wood, Generated Neural Network Function by Matlab, MathWorks, 2016.

[37] MathWorks, Deploy Shallow Neural Network Functions—MATLAB & Simulink, 2020. https://www.mathworks.com/help/deeplearning/ug/deploy-shallow-neural-network-functions-and-objects.html. (Accessed October 31, 2020).

[38] Firehouse, Fire Investigations and Their Role in Prevention, Firehouse, 2007. https://www.firehouse.com/prevention-investigation/article/10494012/fire-investigations-and-their-role-in-prevention. (Accessed September 30, 2020).

[39] G. De Sanctis, Generic Risk Assessment for Fire Safety Performance Evaluation and Optimisation of Design Provisions, 2015, https://doi.org/10.3929/ethz-a-010782581.

[40] A. Cowlard, A. Bittern, C. Abecassis-Empis, J. Torero, Fire safety design for tall buildings, Procedia Eng. 62 (2013) 169–181, https://doi.org/10.1016/j.proeng.2013.08.053.

Application of artificial neural networks in polymer electrolyte membrane fuel cell system prognostics

Lei Mao[a], Kai He[a], Lisa Jackson[b], and Qiang Wu[a]

School of Engineering Science, University of Science and Technology of China, Hefei, China[a] Department of Aeronautical and Automotive Engineering, Loughborough University, Loughborough, United Kingdom[b]

List of acronyms and nomenclature

ANFIS	adaptive neuro-fuzzy inference system
ANN	artificial neural network
BPNN	back propagation neural network
EIS	electrochemical impedance spectroscopy
ESN	echo state network
FinAIR	inlet flow rate of air (l/mn)
FinH$_2$	inlet flow rate of H$_2$ (l/mn)
FoutAIR	outlet flow rate of air (l/mn)
FoutH$_2$	outlet flow rate of H$_2$ (l/mn)
FWAT	flow rate of cooling water (l/mn)
I	current (A)
J	current density (A/cm^2)
LSTM	long short-term memory network
MEA	membrane electrode assemblies
MSE	mean absolute error
N	length of moving window
PEMFC	polymer electrolyte membrane
PinAIR	inlet pressure of air (mbara)
PinH$_2$	inlet pressure of H$_2$ (mbara)
PoutAIR	outlet pressure of air (mbara)
PoutH$_2$	outlet pressure of H$_2$ (mbara)
RMSE	root mean square error
RNN	recurrent neural network
RUL	remaining useful life
SVM	support vector machine
TinAIR	inlet temperatures of air (°C)

Nature-Inspired Computing Paradigms in Systems. https://doi.org/10.1016/B978-0-12-823749-6.00005-2

TinH$_2$	inlet temperatures of H$_2$ (°C)
TinWAT	inlet temperatures of cooling water (°C)
ToutAIR	outlet temperatures of air (°C)
ToutH$_2$	outlet temperatures of H$_2$ (°C)
ToutWAT	outlet temperatures of cooling water (°C)
U1 ~ U5	single cells (V)
Utot	stack voltage (V)
$w_{p,k}$	weight factor
$Y_{eva,k}$	actual voltage at the kth time step
Y_{fus}	fusion results
$y_{pre,p,k}$	pth model prediction voltage value

1. Introduction

As an environmentally friendly and highly efficient energy conversion technique, hydrogen and fuel cell technology has the potential to be an alternative to conventional energy sources, which face rapid energy consumption and environmental deterioration [1]. By the electrochemical reaction, electricity can be provided from fuel gas chemical energy using PEMFC. As shown in Fig. 1, in a typical PEMFC, membrane electrode assemblies (MEAs) are sandwiched using bipolar plates, and sealed by gasket. As a core component, an MEA is manufactured with a proton exchange membrane, anode, and cathode [2, 3]. However, the limited durability is the main issue that hinders the further commercialization of PEMFC. During long-term operation, irreversible membrane material aging and microstructure change will lead to a decrease of PEMFC performance, and even system catastrophe [4]. Moreover, harsh operating conditions such as frequency load cycling and subzero operating temperature will further accelerate PEMFC performance decay [5].

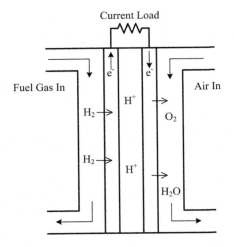

FIG. 1

The structure of a PEMFC.

To address the above issues, prognostic techniques are proposed and applied to PEMFC systems. Through a prognostics approach, the future state of the PEMFC can be estimated with its previous and current data. On such a basis, a PEMFC's remaining useful life (RUL) can be determined, which can facilitate designs of appropriate maintenance strategies [6].

According to previous studies, there are three types of approaches for prognostics: model-driven [7], data-based [8], and hybrid methodologies [9]. For model-driven methods, a model representing a fuel cell system state is constructed based on the empirical experiences or the knowledge of PEMFC, from which state and transition functions can be built. With developed models, various prognostic algorithms, including Kalman filter (KF) [10], particle filter (PF) [11, 12], extended KF [13], and unscented KF [14], can be utilized to predict PEMFC performance and its RUL.

In data-based methods, the machine learning technique is usually utilized to process the information from the PEMFC system, where the corresponding relation between input data and output voltage can be obtained. Data-based approaches are easily implemented, and thus have been widely used in PEMFC prognostics compared with model-driven methods, since an accurate PEMFC system model is difficult to construct. Among different machine learning algorithms, artificial neural network (ANN) [15], adaptive neuro-fuzzy inference system (ANFIS) [16], and support vector machine (SVM) [17] are widely used. Moreover, with improved computation capability, deep learning-based techniques have been applied in PEMFC prognostics, such as recurrent neural network (RNN), echo state network (ESN) [18], and long short-term memory network (LSTM) [19].

As mentioned above, the model-driven method requires the PEMFC system model, while a large amount data is necessary for data-based methods, especially ANN methods. Therefore, hybrid methodologies are proposed to overcome limitations of these two approaches. In hybrid methodologies, model-driven and data-based methods are combined, where outputs from two approaches are fused to provide overall predictions [20]. In some other studies using hybrid methodologies, a model-driven method is used to acquire the PEMFC state, with which data-based approaches can predict the future degradation of PEMFC performance [21].

From previous studies, PEMFC future voltage output can be determined by its historical state as well as its control parameters [22]; thus, both variables associated with PEMFC historical state (like PEMFC previous voltages) and PEMFC system control parameters (such as inlet gas flow rate, pressure, and fuel cell temperature), are used for PEMFC prognostics. However, the effectiveness of these two types of parameters in predicting PEMFC behavior, especially under various operating conditions, has not been investigated, which makes it difficult to choose appropriate parameters for PEMFC prognostics in complex scenarios. Moreover, input parameters in ANN models should also be optimized to provide reliable and efficient predictions for PEMFC systems.

In order to address the mentioned issues, in this chapter, the effects of variables representing the PEMFC previous state and control mode in prognostic analysis are studied in various operating modes. A hybrid approach consisting of the ANFIS and BPNN models is proposed to study the effectiveness of two types of parameters, and to provide reliable predictions under two different operating conditions. Moreover, the correlation-based method is proposed to evaluate correlations between various PEMFC parameters and PEMFC's performance, from which optimal parameters can be determined in PEMFC prognostics. Furthermore, experimental data collected with a PEMFC system are utilized for validating the performance of selected parameters in PEMFC prognosis.

This chapter is structured as follows. The PEMFC test bench and corresponding test data are presented in Section 2. Section 3 presents the proposed hybrid methodologies for PEMFC prognosis, where two widely used models, BPNN and ANFIS, are trained with PEMFC historical state and control parameters, respectively, to provide predictions. Section 4 presents the results of the proposed method in PEMFC prognosis. In Section 5, correlation analysis is firstly introduced, then the correlation co-efficients between parameters representing operating conditions and target output voltage are calculated. With the correlation analysis, a parameter selection method is proposed. Finally, Section 6 provides the conclusions.

2. Description of fuel cell test bench and experimental data

In the aging experiment, two PEMFC stacks are operated with the PEMFC test bench. Each of the stack contains 5-cell with an active area of 100 cm^2. In the test, reactants pass the boiler before reaching the stack, and the boiler can be heated in order to provide the required relative humidity, from which the inlet hygrometry could be estimated. Moreover, a cooling system is used to provide coolants to the stack, where its temperature can be controlled [23]. The first stack is tested under a constant current load (0.7 A/cm^2 for current density), and the second stack is tested using changing current load where high-frequency current ripples are added for simulating the current fluctuations generated by connecting the PEMFC to a static DC/DC converter, which are depicted in Fig. 2A and B, respectively. Voltages of two stacks at different loading conditions are illustrated in Fig. 2C. Moreover, characterization data from electrochemical impedance spectroscopy (EIS) and polarization curve are performed with intervals of about 150 h. With the results from characterization tests, the PEMFC behavior during durability test can be further investigated. Table 1 shows the collection time of characterization test data. More details can be found in [23].

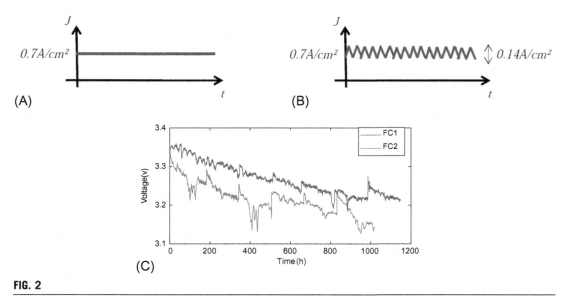

FIG. 2

(A) Constant current density for first stack; (B) varying current density for second stack; (C) PEMFC voltages of first stack and second stack.

Table 1 Characterization time of FC1 and FC2.

FC1	48 h	185 h	348 h	515 h	658 h	823 h	991 h
FC2	35 h	182 h	343 h	515 h	666 h	830 h	1016 h

Table 2 Control parameters gathered during the durability test.

Parameter symbol	Physical meaning
Time	Aging time (h)
U1 $\sim$ U5; Utot	Single cells and stack voltage (V)
I; J	Current (A) and current density (A/cm^2)
TinH$_2$; ToutH$_2$	Inlet and outlet temperatures of H$_2$ (°C)
TinAIR; ToutAIR	Inlet and outlet temperatures of air (°C)
TinWAT; ToutWAT	Inlet and outlet temperatures of cooling water (°C)
PinH$_2$; PoutH$_2$	Inlet and outlet pressure of H$_2$ (mbara)
PinAIR; PoutAIR	Inlet and outlet pressure of air (mbara)
FinH$_2$; FoutH$_2$	Inlet and outlet flow rate of H$_2$ (l/mn)
FinAIR; FoutAIR	Inlet and outlet flow rate of air (l/mn)
FWAT	Flow rate of cooling water (l/mn)

From Fig. 2C, when characterization tests are performed, an abrupt increase of voltage occurs. In order to provide accurate predictions, this phenomenon should be taken into account. Moreover, compared with Fig. 2A, minor variation of current density in Fig. 2B can lead to significant change in corresponding PEMFC voltage, as shown in Fig. 2C, indicating that dynamic loading condition can significantly affect PEMFC performance.

In the test, control parameters are monitored by the sensors of the test bench. Table 2 lists the collected parameters. From Fig. 2C, each stack can operate for more than 1000 h (1155 h for the first stack and 1021 h for the second). Since, in the durability test, PEMFC performance showed a gradual change (as shown in Fig. 2C), it is necessary to resample the test data points with 1 h time interval in the following analysis to save the computational time.

3. A hybrid approach for PEMFC prognosis

In this section, a hybrid approach including BPNN and ANFIS is proposed for predicting PEMFC performance, using both its previous state and control parameters. With the proposed method, the effect of PEMFC previous behavior and control parameters in its prognosis can be clarified.

3.1 Effectiveness evaluation of control parameters with BPNN

An artificial neural network (ANN) is an intelligence method inspired by the way of processing information in the human brain. ANNs have the ability to capture the relation between system inputs and outputs in various applications, which enables them to be widely used in the data processing field [24]. A BPNN is a type of ANN using a back propagation training algorithm for the determination

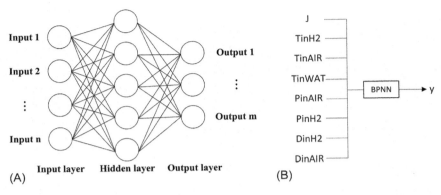

FIG. 3

Structure of BPNN model.

of interconnection weights between neurons in the network [15], which contains three main layers: input, hidden, and output. This is shown in Fig. 3A. It can be observed that layers are fully connected in BPNN, and neurons in the same layer are not connected with each other. In the prognostic process, the prediction error is back-propagated across the network once the prediction from the output layer cannot meet the predefined criteria, and interconnection weights between neurons are adjusted until the predefined criteria are achieved. Considering its easy implementation, the BPNN is utilized for predicting the PEMFC behavior change due to varying loading conditions, where control parameters are changed.

In the analysis, BPNN model is performed for evaluating the effectiveness of control parameters, thus the model inputs data should represent the control parameters, which can be expressed with parameters monitored by sensors (J, TinH$_2$, TinAIR, TinWAT, PinH$_2$, PinAIR, FinH$_2$, and FinAIR, listed in Table 2), while the BPNN model output is PEMFC voltage. This is depicted in Fig. 3B.

In this chapter, BPNN prediction is realized by performing the moving window method, which is effective to deal with a time-dependent problem [25]. The reason for using the moving window is that at each time step with incoming new data, the model will be updated and its predication accuracy will be improved. Moreover, as certain data length is kept in the moving window, old data will be deleted to increase the computation efficiency. In this analysis, the original data set is divided into three subsets with the same length N, including the training part (for training and building prediction models), the evaluation part (for determining the weights for model fusion), and the prediction part (for evaluating model performance), as shown in Fig. 4. With the process of the moving window, new incoming data will be added in the predicting data set for evaluating the model performance, then it will be used as validation data set for calculating the weights for fusion as discussed in Section 3.3, and finally it will be used to train the model. With the further update of the data set, it will be deleted. In brief, each time new data are gathered, old data will be partly deleted to keep the same data length in the moving window, thus the BPNN could be updated continuously. Therefore, with the moving window method, at each step the BPNN will make a prediction with a data length of $3N$ (as shown in Fig. 4, the data length for training, validation, and prediction is the same N).

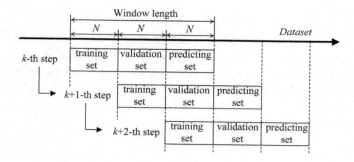

FIG. 4

Moving window method.

3.2 Effectiveness evaluation of historical state with ANFIS

In the study, the effectiveness of fuel cell previous behavior (i.e., stack voltage at previous time steps) in prognosis is evaluated using the ANFIS model, as firstly proposed by Jang et al. [26]. ANFIS combines the neural network and fuzzy inference, giving it learning ability as well as the characterization of fuzzy system [27]. Fig. 5A depicts the structure of the ANFIS model with five layers.

In the ANFIS model, inputs only contain previous stack voltages, while its output is future step voltage. Moreover, the prediction will propagate to the model inputs, thus the model can make predictions iteratively, as shown in Fig. 5B. In this way, ANFIS can predict PEMFC future behavior by learning its historical state. It should be noted that the first 500 h of data will be used to train the ANFIS model, and then the prediction will be iteratively made.

3.3 Proposed hybrid approach

From the above analysis, the effectiveness of PEMFC control parameters and its historical state in prognosis can be evaluated using BPNN and ANFIS, respectively. For this purpose, Eq. (1) is used to fuse the prediction results of two models, and weights of different parameters in PEMFC prognosis can be calculated with Eq. (2).

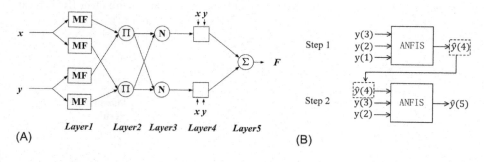

FIG. 5

(A) Structure of the ANFIS model; (B) iterative prediction of the ANFIS model.

$$Y_{fus} = \sum_{p=1}^{2} \frac{w_{p,k}}{\sum w_{p,k}} y_{pre,p,k} \tag{1}$$

where Y_{fus} is the fused result, $y_{pre,p,k}$ is the voltage predicted by the pth model (with $p = 1$ representing the ANFIS model and $p = 2$ the BPNN model, respectively), k represents the prediction time step, and $w_{p,k}$ represents the weight of the pth model at the kth time step.

$$w_{p,k} = \frac{1}{\sqrt{\sum_{i=1}^{N} \left(y_{eva,p,k}(i) - Y_{eva,k}(i) \right)^2}} \tag{2}$$

where $y_{eva,p,k}$ represents the predicted cell voltage from the model at the kth time step and $Y_{eva,k}$ represents the corresponding measured cell voltage. N is the number of predictions results. Since, in the analysis, the moving window method is performed as discussed in Section 3.1, thus the N in Eq. (2) is equal to the data length of each part used in the moving window, as shown in Fig. 4. At the kth time step after training BPNN, the predicted voltages from two models at the validation data set are compared with the actual voltages to calculate the weight factor. As mentioned above, the weight of two models is calculated based on the prediction error. Thus, the model with a lower prediction error will contribute more in the fusion results. Fig. 6 depicts the whole prediction and prediction process with the hybrid prognostic technique.

4. Effectiveness of proposed hybrid approach in PEMFC predictions

In this section, the effectiveness of PEMFC previous behavior and operating mode in the prognosis at both static and quasistatic conditions will be evaluated using the hybrid approach. Furthermore, the importance of parameters selection in the prognostic is studied.

4.1 Effectiveness of the proposed hybrid approach at static operating condition

The original data are resampled with a sampling period of 1 h to save the training time without affecting the accuracy of prediction results in the analysis. As mentioned above, the moving window method is performed in the prediction, thus the window length N should be determined for the BPNN. For qualifying the prediction performance of the BPNN model, the root mean square error (RMSE) and mean absolute error (MAE) are selected, which are expressed in Eqs. (3) and (4).

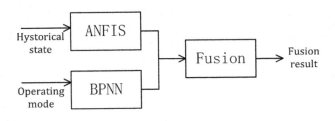

FIG. 6

Flow chart of prediction and fusion process.

$$\text{RMSE} = \sqrt{\frac{1}{m}\sum_{i=1}^{m}(\hat{y}_i - y_i)^2} \qquad (3)$$

$$\text{MAE} = \frac{1}{m}\sum_{i=1}^{m}|\hat{y}_i - y_i| \qquad (4)$$

where y_i represents the actual voltage and $\hat{y}_i$ is the corresponding prediction, and m represents the number of data points.

Fig. 7 depicts the effect of N on RMSE and computational time, where 500 h of data are used in the training. From Fig. 7, the results show that with the increase of N, the computational time reduces while a lower prediction accuracy would be obtained. In order to achieve a desirable level of accuracy without using too much computational time, N is selected to be 10.

From Fig. 7, the computational cost will be decreased with increasing N. The reason is that in the analysis, model training takes up the main computational time and effort. As N is the data length used in training (as shown in Fig. 4), the longer the training data length is, the less models need to be trained (since the whole data length is certain). Therefore, with increased N, the computational time will be decreased. For example, if the window length ($3N$) is equal to the whole data length, then only one BPNN model should be trained, leading to minimal training time.

Moreover, it should be noted that at steady-state condition, the selection of N will not significantly affect training time and prediction accuracy (as shown in Fig. 7), but this will become more obvious at dynamic condition. Even at PEMFC2 in this chapter where minor dynamics is used, the effect of N will be different (RMSE is 0.0090 for $N = 5$ and 0.0309 for $N = 50$). It is expected that with more dynamic load, more significant influence of N will be provided.

Moreover, in the analysis, two PEMFC stacks operated about 1000 h in the durability test, and without significant dynamic load, sampling frequency of 1 h/sample is used herein. In practical application with more complicated dynamic load, longer operating time may be experienced with higher sampling frequency, and N should be carefully selected in order to provide efficient predictions.

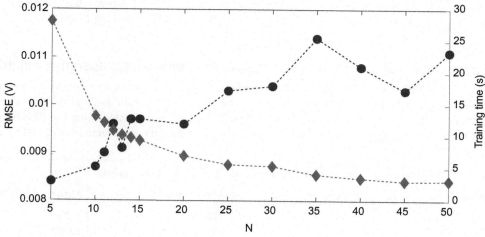

FIG. 7

RMSE and computational time under different window lengths.

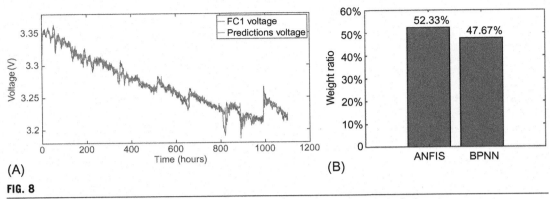

FIG. 8

(A) Hybrid prediction results on first stack; (B) average weight of two models in fusion step.

Moreover, as shown in Fig. 2D, the abrupt voltage jump that occurred when characterization is operated should be considered in the prognosis. Since this voltage jump effect is due to the characterization test and cannot be predicted by the neural network, an empirical voltage jump model is used to reduce the prediction error. More details can be found in [11].

Fig. 8A depicts prediction results with the proposed hybrid technique, while Fig. 8B depicts the weight ratio of two models in the fusion process. Table 3 lists the prediction errors of the fusion method and two individual models.

From Table 3, better PEMFC predictions can be provided using ANFIS at static operation condition. The reason is that PEMFC system control parameters are kept constant in this scenario, thus PEMFC future performance is determined mainly by its previous state. Since the effectiveness of PEMFC previous behavior is evaluated by ANFIS, it has a higher average weight than BPNN.

Furthermore, prediction results from the proposed hybrid method show little improvement compared to the predictions from ANFIS, but compared to results from BPNN using control parameters, the hybrid approach can provide clearly better predictions. This further confirms that accurate prediction can be acquired from only using PEMFC previous behavior, at static operating condition.

4.2 Effectiveness of proposed hybrid approach at Quasistatic operating condition

From Fig. 2D, the PEMFC degradation trend is complex and not linear at dynamic condition, leading to difficulties in predicting PEMFC future voltages. Similar to Section 4.1, in this section, the effectiveness of PEMFC control parameters as well as previous behavior are evaluated using the BPNN model and ANFIS model, respectively. In the analysis, 500 h of training data are selected for model training,

Table 3 RMSEs and MAEs of the fusion technique and individual models.			
First STACK	**BPNN model**	**ANFIS model**	**Fusion technique**
RMSE (V)	0.0139	0.0080	0.0079
MAE (V)	0.0088	0.0058	0.0055

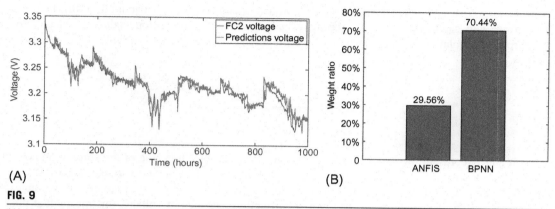

(A)

(B)

FIG. 9

(A) Hybrid prediction results on second stack; (B) average weight of two models in fusion step.

while the rest are utilized for validation. Moreover, the optimal N determined in Section 4.1 (10 herein) is used in the following analysis.

Fig. 9A depicts overall prediction with the hybrid method, while the weight ratios of two models in the fusion process are shown in Fig. 9B, where the average weight of the BPNN model using control parameters is higher than that of ANFIS. In Table 4, the prediction accuracy of the hybrid method and individual methods is compared. The results show that more accurate predictions can be provided with control parameters from the BPNN, which shows significant difference to that at steady-state condition. Moreover, with the hybrid approach, the prediction accuracy can be further improved. From the results, accurate PEMFC degradation prediction can be obtained by utilizing both parameters representing PMEFC historical behavior and control parameters, especially at dynamic operating condition.

5. Input parameter optimization using correlation-based analysis

In this section, correlation-based analysis is performed to investigate correlations between various parameters and PEMFC output voltage. From the results, optimal parameters can be determined to provide accurate predictions using fewer sensor parameters.

5.1 Correlation-based analysis

From the results in Section 4, it can be found that with different inputs, various predictions can be provided using ANN models, indicating that different parameters can make various contributions in

Table 4 RMSEs and MAEs of the fusion technique and individual model.			
Second STACK	**BPNN model**	**ANFIS model**	**Fusion technique**
RMSE (V)	0.0166	0.0346	0.0123
MAE (V)	0.0106	0.0270	0.0091

PEMFC prognosis. Therefore, it is necessary to evaluate each parameter contribution, from which optimal parameters can be determined in the analysis. In this chapter, correlation analysis is selected for this purpose. Correlation analysis calculates the correlation coefficient of two variables (u, v), shown in Eq. (5):

$$Cor(U, V) = \frac{\sum\limits_{i=1}^{n}(u_i - \bar{u})(v_i - \bar{v})}{\sqrt{\sum\limits_{i=1}^{n}(u_i - \bar{u})^2 \sum\limits_{i=1}^{n}(v_i - \bar{v})^2}} \tag{5}$$

where $\bar{u}$ and $\bar{v}$ represent the mean values of u and v, respectively. The value of the correlation coefficient is in the interval of $[-1.1]$. A value of 1 or -1 indicates that the two variables have a strong relationship, while a value closes to 0 means that a weak relationship exists between the two variables [28]. For example, if one parameter has a high correlation with output voltage, this means that this parameter is important to the prediction.

5.2 Effectiveness of correlation-based analysis in PEMFC prognosis

In the study, the correlation coefficient of various control parameters to PEMFC output is calculated. With the results, control parameters can be ranked based on their correlations.

Table 5 lists calculated correlations between various control parameters (sensors listed in Table 2) and PEMFC output voltage. The rank is reasonable and can be explained using PEMFC working behavior at different loading conditions. The sensor J represents the current load; since it can directly affect the output voltage, it has a higher rank in FC1 and FC2.

Moreover, different ranks can be observed for other parameters at different operating conditions. For FC1, as steady-state condition is used, several control parameters, such as gas pressure and flow rate, are kept constant, thus will not affect PEMFC voltage, where lower ranks can be observed for these parameters. On the other side, with dynamic load used in FC2, gas pressures will be changed based on the current, thus they can clearly affect the PEMFC voltage; therefore, in this scenario, higher ranks for gas pressures can be obtained. Therefore, the results obtained in Table 5 are consistent with physical PEMFC behavior at different operating conditions.

It can be seen that different ranks can be obtained at various PEMFC operating conditions, where TinWAT is most related to PEMFC output at steady-state condition (FC1), while the best correlated parameter is changed to TinAIR at dynamic condition (FC2). This indicates the robustness of the

Table 5 Correlation coefficients and ranks of sensors under two operation modes.

Sensor symbol	J	TinH$_2$	TinAIR	TinWAT	PinAIR	PinH$_2$	FinH$_2$	FinAIR
FC1	−0.3179	−0.5605	0.2607	0.6020	0.1904	0.0628	0.2431	0.1374
Rank	3	2	4	1	6	8	5	7
FC2	−0.2901	−0.6442	−0.7082	0.2090	−0.3008	−0.1355	−0.0608	−0.1450
Rank	4	2	1	5	3	7	8	6

proposed correlation-based method, as different parameters better correlated to PEMFC behavior can be determined at various PEMFC applications, which is consistent with results in the previous section, where different types of inputs (PEMFC historical behavior or control parameters) should be used to provide reliable performance predictions at various operating conditions.

Furthermore, the BPNN is utilized to investigate the effect of ranked parameters on prognosis, where parameter set for prognosis is increased one by one based on the rank listed in Table 5. Fig. 10 depicts a flowchart of using the BPNN for determining optimal parameters in PEMFC prognosis.

With the flowchart shown in Fig. 10, the prediction accuracy and training time of the BPNN model using different parameter sets under both different operating conditions are investigated. It should be noted that in each step, 10 BPNN models are trained. Fig. 11 shows the results, where prediction accuracy is evaluated using RMSE in Eq. (3).

At steady-state condition (Fig. 11A), training time decreases with an increase of sensor number, indicating that with more useful information contained in model inputs, the BPNN could reach convergence more efficiently. However, with a further increase of parameter number (4 in this case), training time will be increased accordingly. This turning point can be used when selecting appropriate parameters in the prognosis, as the addition of these parameters providing redundant information will make it difficult for the model to reach convergence. This can also be confirmed with the RMSE curve with different parameters shown in Fig. 11A, where lower RMSE can be obtained by adding parameters with higher correlation—that is, parameters making positive contributions to PEMFC prognosis—while with the addition of parameters with lower correlations and containing redundant information, RMSE will increase. It should be mentioned that this tuning point is the same to the tuning point of the

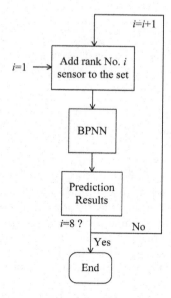

FIG. 10

Flow chart of the prediction process.

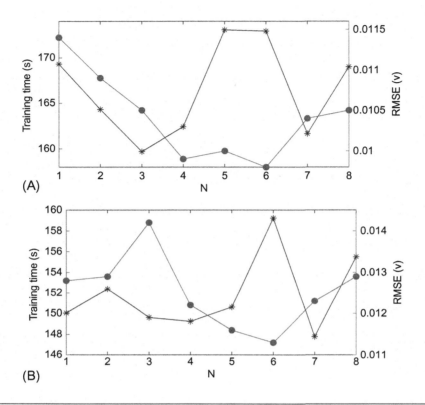

FIG. 11

(A) BPNN prediction accuracy and training cost using different number of sensors at static operation condition;
(B) BPNN prediction accuracy and training cost using different numbers of sensors at quasistatic operation condition.

training time evolution curve. Therefore, by considering both training time and prediction accuracy, four parameters (J, TinH$_2$, TinAIR, and TinWAT) should be used for PEMFC prognosis at steady-state condition.

At quasistatic condition, it can be seen that when adding the last three sensors (PinH$_2$, FinH$_2$, and FinAIR in Table 5) in PEMFC prognosis, both training time and prediction error start to increase, indicating that the last three sensors with smaller correlation coefficients will not contribute to PEMFC prognosis. Similar to that in the steady-state scenario, the tuning point in the training time and RMSE curves can be used for determining the optimal parameter number. As shown in Fig. 11B, with an increase of the parameter number from one to five, the BPNN model can reach convergence more efficiently, while lower RMSE can be observed. Therefore, five sensors (J, TinH$_2$, TinAIR, TinWAT, and PinAIR in Table 5) should be used in PEMFC future voltage prediction at dynamic condition, as shown in Fig. 2C.

From the above results, it can be concluded that correlation coefficients between various parameters and PEMFC output voltage can be used as a baseline for selecting appropriate parameters for PEMFC prognosis, where the optimal parameter number can be determined with the BPNN with the flowchart depicted in Fig. 10. This will be beneficial in practical applications to determine proper variables in PEMFC prognosis, meaning that accurate PEMFC predictions can be made more efficiently.

6. Conclusion

In this chapter, the effects of PEMFC previous behavior and its control parameters on its prognosis at various operating modes were evaluated by the BPNN and ANFIS, respectively. For investigating the effectiveness of each factor, a hybrid technique was proposed, from which the weight representing the contribution of the individual model was calculated. Furthermore, correlation analysis was performed to evaluate correlations between PEMFC control parameters and its performance. By eliminating parameters having less correlation with PEMFC performance, PEMFC prognosis can be further improved, while less computational time is required.

With the proposed hybrid prognostic approach, PEMFC historical behavior and control parameters show different effectiveness on PEMFC prognosis at various operating modes. At steady-state condition, PEMFC performance is mainly determined by its previous behavior. While at quasistatic condition, PEMFC control parameters have significant influence on PEMFC performance, thus the PEMFC control parameters should be considered in prognosis. Moreover, with the hybrid method, accurate PEMFC prognostic performance can be provided at different operating conditions.

Furthermore, optimal parameters are selected by evaluating correlation coefficients between these parameters and PEMFC output, and the effectiveness of selected parameters in PEMFC prognosis is investigated using the BPNN. The results show that with higher correlation parameters in PEMFC prognosis, prediction accuracy can be improved, while prognostic results will be reduced by adding parameters having lower correlations, i.e., parameters with redundant information.

According to the above analysis, when performing prognosis for PEMFC, different control parameters should be taken into account based on the operating modes. With correlation analysis, reliable future degradation predictions at various operating modes can be realized using parameters with higher correlations. From the findings, maintenance strategies can be designed for extending PEMFC lifespan. In the study, experimental data from the PEMFC stack operating under static and quasistatic conditions were utilized for evaluating the proposed method. In future studies, the proposed method will be performed at more complicated operating conditions, such as practical applications. Furthermore, more advanced neural network-related methods, such as long short-term memory network (LSTM) and echo state network (ESN), will be used in order to provide more accurate results.

References

[1] E.A. Wargo, C.R. Dennison, E.C. Kumbur, Polymer Electrolyte Fuel Cell Degradation, Academic, 2012.
[2] W.R.W. Daud, R.E. Rosli, E.H. Majlan, S.A.A. Hamid, R. Mohamed, T. Husaini, PEM fuel cell system control: a review, Renew. Energy 113 (2017) 620–638.
[3] N. Ishiguro, T. Saida, T. Uruga, O. Sekizawa, K. Nagasawa, K. Nitta, T. Yamamoto, S. Ohkoshi, T. Yokoyama, M. Tada, Structural kinetics of a Pt/C cathode catalyst with practical catalyst loading in an MEA for PEFC operating conditions studied by in situ time-resolved XAFS, Phys. Chem. Chem. Phys. 15 (2013) 18827–18834.

[4] L. Dubau, L. Castanheira, F. Maillard, M. Chatenet, O. Lottin, G. Maranzana, J. Dillet, A. Lamibrac, J.-.C. Perrin, E. Moukheiber, A. ElKaddouri, G. De Moor, C. Bas, L. Flandin, N. Caqué, A review of PEM fuel cell durability: materials degradation, local heterogeneities of aging and possible mitigation strategies, WIREs. Energy. Environ. 3 (2014) 540–560.

[5] Q. Li, H. Yang, Y. Han, M. Li, W. Chen, A state machine strategy based on droop control for an energy management system of PEMFC-battery-supercapacitor hybrid tramway, Int. J. Hydrogen Energy 41 (36) (2016) 16148–16159.

[6] M. Jouin, R. Gouriveau, D. Hissel, M.C. Péra, N. Zerhouni, Prognostics and health management of PEMFC—state of the art and remaining challenges, Int. J. Hydrogen Energy 38 (35) (2013) 15307–15317.

[7] E. Lechartier, R. Gouriveau, M.C. Pera, D. Hissel, N. Zerhouni, Static and dynamic modeling of a PEMFC for prognostics purpose, in: Proc. IEEE Veh. Power Propulsion Conf., Coimbra, Portugal, 2014, pp. 1–5.

[8] N. Laayouj, H. Jamouli, Remaining useful life prediction of lithium-ion battery degradation for a hybrid electric vehicle, Global Adv. Res. J. Eng., Technol. Innov. 4 (2) (2015) 16–23.

[9] K. Javed, R. Gouriveau, N. Zerhouni, P. Nectoux, Enabling health monitoring approach based on vibration data for accurate prognostics, IEEE Trans. Ind. Electron. 62 (1) (Jan. 2015) 647–656.

[10] J.K. Kimotho, T. Meyer, W. Sextro, PEM fuel cell prognostics using particle filter with model parameter adaptation, in: 2014 International Conference on Prognostics and Health Management, Cheney, WA, 2014, pp. 1–6.

[11] D. Zhang, C. Cadet, C. Bérenguer, N.Y. Steiner, Some improvements of particle filtering based prognosis for PEM fuel cells, IFAC-PapersOnLine 49 (28) (2016) 162–167.

[12] L. Mao, L. Jackson, T. Jackson, Investigation of polymer electrolyte membrane fuel cell internal behaviour during long term operation and its use in prognostics, J. Power Sources 362 (2017) 39–49.

[13] M. Bressel, M. Hilairet, D. Hissel, B.O. Bouamama, Extended Kalman filter for prognostic of proton exchange membrane fuel cell, Appl. Energy 164 (2016) 220–227.

[14] H. Liu, J. Chen, C. Zhu, H. Su, M. Hou, Prognostics of proton exchange membrane fuel cells using a model-based method, IFAC-PapersOnLine 50 (1) (2017) 4757–4762.

[15] M. Seyhan, Y.E. Akansu, M. Murat, Y. Korkmaz, S.O. Akansu, Performance prediction of PEM fuel cell with wavy serpentine flow channel by using artificial neural network, Int. J. Hydrogen Energy 42 (40) (2017) 25619–25629.

[16] L. Mao, L. Jackson, Selection of optimal sensors for predicting performance polymer electrolyte membrane fuel cell, J. Power Sources 328 (2016) 151–160.

[17] A. Kheirandish, N. Shafiabady, M. Dahari, M.S. Kazemi, D. Isa, Modeling of commercial proton exchange membrane fuel cell using support vector machine, Int. J. Hydrogen Energy 41 (26) (2016) 11351–11358.

[18] Z. Hua, Z. Zheng, M.-C. Péra, F. Gao, Remaining useful life prediction of PEMFC systems based on the multi-input echo state network, Appl. Energy 265 (2020) 114791.

[19] J. Liu, Q. Li, W. Chen, Y. Yan, Y. Qiu, T. Cao, Remaining useful life prediction of PEMFC based on long short-term memory recurrent neural networks, Int. J. Hydrogen Energy 44 (11) (2019) 5470–5480.

[20] D. Zhou, F. Gao, E. Breaz, A. Ravey, A. Miraoui, Degradation prediction of PEM fuel cell using a moving window based hybrid prognostic approach, Energy 138 (2017) 1175–1186.

[21] H. Liu, J. Chen, D. Hissel, H. Su, Remaining useful life estimation for proton exchange membrane fuel cells using a hybrid method, Appl. Energy 237 (2019) 910–919.

[22] J. Wu, et al., A review of PEM fuel cell durability: degradation mechanisms and mitigation strategies, J. Power Sources 184 (1) (2008) 104–119.

[23] FCLAB research, IEEE PHM Data Challenge 2014, 2014. http://eng.fclab.fr/ieee-phm-2014-data-challenge/.

[24] Y. Bicer, I. Dincer, M. Aydin, Maximizing performance of fuel cell using artificial neural network approach for smart grid applications, Energy 116 (1) (2016) 1205–1217.

[25] M.N. Kashani, J. Aminian, S. Shahhosseini, M. Farrokhi, Dynamic crude oil fouling prediction in industrial preheaters using optimized ANN based moving window technique, Chem. Eng. Res. Des. 90 (7) (2012) 938–949.

[26] J.-R. Jang, ANFIS: adaptive-network-based fuzzy inference system, IEEE Trans. Syst. Man Cybern. 23 (3) (1993) 665–685.

[27] K.J. Reddy, N. Sudhakar, ANFIS-MPPT control algorithm for a PEMFC system used in electric vehicle applications, Int. J. Hydrogen Energy 44 (29) (2019) 15355–15369.

[28] H. Leng, X. Li, J. Zhu, H. Tang, Z. Zhang, N. Ghadimi, A new wind power prediction method based on ridgelet transforms, hybrid feature selection and closed-loop forecasting, Adv. Eng. Inform. 36 (2018) 20–30.

Reliability redundancy allocation problems under fuzziness using genetic algorithm and dual-connection numbers

Laxminarayan Sahoo

Department of Computer and Information Science, Raiganj University, Raiganj, India

1. Introduction

Because of the advancement of the latest technological systems, the configuration of a system is tremendously dependent on the choice of components, and hence system reliability is a key count to be examined in system management. When implementing a desirable system, one question comes to the fore regarding the balance between the system reliability and other physical parameters, viz. cost, volume, and weight. To study the reliability redundancy allocation problem (RRAP), the problem relating to the bridge network system has been formulated as an integer constrained optimization problem. The main goals of the RRAP are to maximize the system reliability under several budget constraints and also to determine the comprehensive reliability of a system by optimal assignment of redundancy components in the whole system. The reliability of a bridge network system might be refined by adding identical or some nonidentical parts/elements to each subsystem as design frameworks. For a system with some fixed constraints and other parameters associated with that system, the equivalent design problem is categorized as a combinatorial optimization problem, design problem is called/design problem is called an RRAP. Because of the highly nonlinear and complex nature of the RRAP, the problem cannot be resolved by direct/indirect or mixed search optimization techniques due to the discontinuous solution domain of the problem. The RRAP has been competently analyzed by Tillman et al. [1] and Kuo and Prasad [2]. In the existing areas of research, it has been seen that diverse techniques—viz. heuristic [3–6], branch and bound method [7–9], reduced gradient technique [10], integer programming [11], dynamic programming (DP) [12, 13], etc.—were employed to solve such an RRAP. Although these techniques have a few merits, they also have drawbacks. DP cannot be applied for solving complex problems as the latter are unable to be broken down into equivalent subproblems. In the branch and bound method, the efficacy of the methods determined by the acuteness of the bound and space complexity rises rapidly with the size of the problem. Thence, with the advent of the genetic algorithm [14] and some other heuristic/meta-heuristic optimization algorithms, a good number of scientific experts in

Nature-Inspired Computing Paradigms in Systems. https://doi.org/10.1016/B978-0-12-823749-6.00003-9

this area have been inspired to apply these methods/techniques to solve the RRAP. Garg [15] proposed a biogeography-based optimization technique controlled by a penalty function for solving RRAPs of series-parallel systems under several budget constraints. Garg [16] also developed a cuckoo search (CS) optimization technique to obtain the finest solution of the RRAP considering some nonlinear constraints. Using particle swarm optimization (PSO), the RRAP for series-parallel has been well studied by Garg et al. [17]. Garg and Sharma [18] have also solved multiple objective RRAPs by use of PSO. Garg et al. [19] proposed a two-phase technique for solving the RRAP with nonlinear resource constraints using an artificial bee colony (ABC) optimization technique. These methods provide more versatility (i.e., they do not depend on any assumption of linearity, separability, or convexity, and need one or two premises on the objective as well as restrictions of the problem and very simple to contrive). These methods are very methodical even if the solution domain is continuous and/or discontinuous.

In previous work, the limiting factors of most of the RRAPs have generally been taken to be precise values and hence complete information about the system is perceived. However, in reality there are no adequate statistical inputs available for most of the engineering design systems, and precise statistics about the system cannot be cumulated due to human errors and other unexpected characteristics relating to the environment. Thus, system parameters will be viewed as imprecise. In this case, fuzzy set theory plays a starring role to handle such vague parameters [20]. Regarding reliability optimization with imprecise/vague parameters, one may mention the studies of Gupta et al. [21], Sahoo et al. [22], Bhunia et al. [23], and Garg et al. [24].

In this chapter, we have managed imprecise/vague parameters in view of fuzzy numbers. Hence, the fuzzy valued RRAP furnishes a systematic order scheme that solves the optimization problem with fuzzy valued parameters. To find optimal system reliability, the corresponding optimization problem has been transformed to an interval valued optimization problem by making use of dual-connection numbers (DCNs) [25] of fuzzy parameters. DCNs have been extensively used in a large number of areas to keep up decision-makers (DMs) in promising, suitable, and reasonable perceptions. For details about DCNs, the reader is referred to the current research works of Garg and Kumar [26, 27] and Fu and Zhou [28]. Here, we have used DCNs because they can easily handle uncertainty/imprecise parameters [26–28].

In this chapter, we have successfully applied the genetic algorithm (GA) to find the most favorable solution of the RRAP of a five-link bridge network where all the parameters relating to the problem are imprecise. The triangular fuzzy number (TFN) is applied to represent the impreciseness of the parameters. Moreover, dual-connection numbers (DCNs) have been taken into consideration as they can easily handle impreciseness. Using DCNs, we have converted the TFN to its corresponding interval number.

Therefore, the objective of this chapter is to discuss a solution procedure for resolving the RRAP of a five-link bridge network with imprecise parameters in which parameters are taken as imprecise/vague by means of TFNs. The solution procedure is based on DCNs of fuzzy parameters and use of real coded GA. The proposed method is illustrated at the end of the chapter using a hypothetical numerical example. Subsequently, the formulated problem has been transformed to an optimization problem where the objective function and constraints of the problem are in terms of intervals. Using the Big-M penalty technique [21, 23], the constrained interval optimization problem has been transformed to an unconstrained one with interval coefficients. Real coded GA is used to find out the solution of the problem. Finally, to demonstrate the proposed approach, an example has been solved and the computed solutions have been furnished.

2. Prerequisite mathematics

A fuzzy set is originated by Zadeh [20] in a scientific manner to represent impreciseness or vagueness in our daily life.

Fuzzy set: A fuzzy set $\widetilde{A}$ is defined as the set of pairs $\widetilde{A} = \{(x, \mu_{\widetilde{A}}(x)) : x \in X\}$, where $\mu_{\widetilde{A}} : X \to [0, 1]$ is a mapping and $\mu_{\widetilde{A}}(x)$ is called the membership function of $\widetilde{A}$.

α-cut: The α-cut of a fuzzy set $\widetilde{A}$ is a subset of X defined by $\widetilde{A}_{\alpha} = \{x \in X : \mu_{\widetilde{A}}(x) \geq \alpha\}$, where $\mu_{\widetilde{A}}(x)$ is the membership function of $\widetilde{A}$ and $\alpha \in [0, 1]$.

Normal fuzzy set: A fuzzy set $\widetilde{A}$ is called normal if there exists at least one $x \in X$ such that $\mu_{\widetilde{A}}(x) = 1$.

Convex fuzzy set: A fuzzy set $\widetilde{A}$ is called convex iff for $x_1, x_2 \in X$, $\mu_{\widetilde{A}}(x)$ satisfies the inequality $\mu_{\widetilde{A}}(\lambda x_1 + (1 - \lambda)x_2) \geq \min\{\mu_{\widetilde{A}}(x_1), \mu_{\widetilde{A}}(x_2)\}$, where $\lambda \in [0, 1]$.

Triangular fuzzy number: The TFN is denoted as $\widetilde{A} = (a_l, a_m, a_u)$, where $a_l \leq a_m \leq a_u$ and its membership function $\mu_{\widetilde{A}}(x) : X \to [0, 1]$ is defined by:

$$\mu_{\widetilde{A}}(x) = \begin{cases} \dfrac{x - a_l}{a_m - a_l} & \text{if } a_l \leq x \leq a_m \\ 1 & \text{if } x = a_m \\ \dfrac{a_u - x}{a_u - a_m} & \text{if } a_m \leq x \leq a_u \\ 0 & \text{otherwise} \end{cases}$$

Dual connection number: Suppose that $x, y, z \in \mathbb{R}^+$ and $\theta \in [-1, 1]$, $\delta = -1$, then $v = x + y\theta + z\delta$ is a similar disparity opposing a three-component connection number. When $z = 0$, then $v = x + y\theta$ is a similar different DCN, and when $x + y + z = 1$, then $v = x + y\theta + z\delta$ is a normalized similar disparity category three-component connection number.

Now, here we shall give some arithmetic operations of connection numbers, which are as follows: Let $v_1 = x_1 + y_1\theta$ and $v_2 = x_2 + y_2\theta$ be two identical connection numbers, then:

(i) $v_1 + v_2 = (x_1 + x_2) + \theta(y_1 + y_2)$
(ii) $v_1 - v_2 = (x_1 - x_2) + \theta(y_1 - y_2)$
(iii) $v_1 v_2 = x_1 x_2 + \theta(x_1 y_2 + y_1 x_2 + y_1 y_2)$

Definition 1. (Irvanizam et al. [25]) If $\widetilde{A} = (a_1, a_2, a_3)$ is a TFN, then the DCN of $\widetilde{A}$ is $u_{\widetilde{A}} = p_{\widetilde{A}} + q_{\widetilde{A}}\theta$, where $p_{\widetilde{A}} = a_2$ and $q_{\widetilde{A}} = \dfrac{\sqrt{(a_2 - a_1)^2 + (a_2 - a_3)^2}}{2}$, $\theta \in [-1, 1]$.

Definition 2. (Irvanizam et al. [25]) If $\widetilde{A} = (a_1, a_2, a_3)$ is a TFN, then $u = [u_L, u_R]$ is the corresponding interval number where $u_L = p_{\widetilde{A}} - q_{\widetilde{A}}$ and $u_R = p_{\widetilde{A}} + q_{\widetilde{A}}$.

Definition 3. (Moore [29]; Moore, Kearfott, and Cloud [30]) An interval number is denoted by $A = [a_L, a_R]$ and is defined by $A = [a_L, a_R] = \{a : a_L \leq a \leq a_R, a \in \mathbb{R}\}$, where a_L and a_R are the lower and upper bounds, respectively, and $\mathbb{R}$ is the set of real numbers.

Alternatively, an interval A can also be exhibited as $A = \langle a_c, a_w \rangle$, where $a_c = (a_L + a_R)/2$ and $a_w = (a_R - a_L)/2$ are the center and radius of the interval A, respectively.

Definition 4. (Moore, Kearfott, and Cloud [30]; Hansen and Walster [31]) Let $A = [a_L, a_R] = \langle a_c, a_w \rangle$ and $B = [b_L, b_R] = \langle b_c, b_w \rangle$ be two interval numbers in R. We define:

$$A + B = \begin{cases} (i) & [a_L + b_L, a_R + b_R] \text{ or} \\ (ii) & \langle a_c + b_c, a_w + b_w \rangle \end{cases}$$

$$A - B = \begin{cases} (i) & [a_L - b_R, a_R - b_L] \text{ or} \\ (ii) & \langle a_c - b_c, a_w + b_w \rangle \end{cases}$$

$$\lambda A = \begin{cases} (i) & \begin{cases} [\lambda a_L, \lambda a_R] & \text{if } \lambda \geq 0 \\ [\lambda a_R, \lambda a_L] & \text{if } \lambda < 0 \end{cases} \text{ or} \\ (ii) & \langle \lambda a_c, |\lambda| a_w \rangle \end{cases}$$

$$A \times B = [\min(a_L b_L, a_L b_R, a_R b_L, a_R b_R), \max(a_L b_L, a_L b_R, a_R b_L, a_R b_R)]$$

$$\frac{B}{A} = B \times \frac{1}{A} = [b_L, b_R] \times \left[\frac{1}{a_R}, \frac{1}{a_L}\right], \text{provided } 0 \notin [a_L, a_R].$$

If n is any nonnegative integer, then the integral power of an interval [32] can be defined as:

$$A^n = \begin{cases} [1, 1] & \text{if } n = 0 \\ [a_L^n, a_R^n] & \text{if } a_L \geq 0 \text{ or if } n \text{ is odd} \\ [a_R^n, a_L^n] & \text{if } a_R \leq 0 \text{ and } n \text{ is even} \\ [0, \max(a_L^n, a_R^n)] & \text{if } a_L \leq 0 \leq a_R \text{ and } n(> 0) \text{ is even.} \end{cases}$$

Again, to achieve the optimum solution of interval valued decision problems, the ranking of interval numbers is essential. Between two interval numbers $A = [a_L, a_R]$ and $B = [b_L, b_R]$, there are three types of relations [33], as follows:

(i) Two intervals are nonoverlapping.
(ii) Two intervals are partially overlapping.
(iii) One of the intervals contains the other one (inclusion).

It should be noted that two intervals $A = [a_L, a_R]$ and $B = [b_L, b_R]$ will be the same in the case of fully overlapping intervals (i.e., $A = B$ iff $a_L = b_L$ and $a_R = b_R$).

Definition 5. (Sahoo et al. [22]) Let $A = [a_L, a_R] = \langle a_c, a_w \rangle$ and $B = [b_L, b_R] = \langle b_c, b_w \rangle$ be two interval numbers. If $>_{\max}$ is the order relation between the intervals A and B, then for maximization problems:

$$A >_{\max} B \Leftrightarrow \begin{cases} (i) \, a_c > b_c \text{ for Type} - 1 \text{ and Type} - 2 \text{ intervals or} \\ (ii) \text{ either } a_c \geq b_c \wedge a_w < b_w \text{ or } a_c \geq b_c \wedge a_R > b_R \text{ for Type} - 3 \text{ intervals} \end{cases}$$

Definition 6. Sahoo et al. [22]) Let $A = [a_L, a_R] = \langle a_c, a_w \rangle$ and $B = [b_L, b_R] = \langle b_c, b_w \rangle$ be two interval numbers. If $<_{\min}$ is the order relation between the intervals A and B, then for minimization problems:

$$A <_{\min} B \Leftrightarrow \begin{cases} (i) \, a_c > b_c \text{ for Type} - 1 \text{ and Type} - 2 \text{ intervals or} \\ (ii) \text{ either } a_c \leq b_c \wedge a_w < b_w \text{ or } a_c \leq b_c \wedge a_L < b_L \text{ for Type} - 3 \text{ intervals} \end{cases}$$

3. Problem formulation: Reliability redundancy allocation problem (RRAP)

An RRAP has been formulated under the following notations:

3.1 Notations

R_S Overall system reliability;

x_j Number of redundancies in the jth subsystems;

R_j The jth subsystem reliability with respect to x_j;

f The system reliability function;

g_i The total consumption of ith resource for allocation $(x_1, x_2, ..., x_n)$;

b_i The total amount of ith resource available;

l_j Lower integer limit of x_j; and

u_j Upper integer limit of x_j.

Think about a bridge network system comprising n subsystems and m constraints. The basic objective of this problem is to determine the number of optimal components in each of the subsystems to maximize the all-inclusive system reliability depending on the prescribed limitations upon budgets/resources. This problem can be written as an integer nonlinear programming problem (INLPP), which is as follows:

$$\text{Maximize} \, R_S = f(x_1, x_2, ..., x_n) = h(R_1(x_1), R_2(x_2), ..., R_n(x_n)) \tag{1}$$

subject to

$$g_i(x_1, x_2, ..., x_n) \leq b_i, \text{ for } i = 1, 2, ..., m$$

$$1 \leq l_j \leq x_j \leq u_j, \text{ for } j = 1, ..., n,$$

When all the parameters are under fuzziness, then the problem (1) is reduced to:

$$\text{Maximize} \, \tilde{R}_S = \tilde{f}(x_1, x_2, ..., x_n) = h(\tilde{R}_1(x_1), \tilde{R}_2(x_2), ..., \tilde{R}_n(x_n)) \tag{2}$$

subject to:

$$\tilde{g}_i(x_1, x_2, ..., x_n) \leq \tilde{b}_i, \text{ for } i = 1, 2, ..., m$$

$$1 \leq l_j \leq x_j \leq u_j, \text{ for } j = 1, ..., n,$$

where $\tilde{R}_S$, $\tilde{g}_i$, and $\tilde{b}_i$ are all fuzzy valued system reliability, ith constraint, and ith resource, respectively. Now if the parameters of problem (2) are TFNs, then using DCNs of fuzzy numbers, the same problem can be transformed into an interval valued constrained optimization problem. Thus, the corresponding problem can be written as follows:

$$\text{Maximize} \, \tilde{R}_S = [R_{SL}, R_{SR}] \tag{3}$$

subject to:

$$[g_{iL}, g_{iR}] \leq [b_{iL}, b_{iR}], \text{ for } i = 1, 2, ..., m$$

$$1 \leq l_j \leq x_j \leq u_j, \text{ for } j = 1, ..., n,$$

where $[R_{SL}, R_{SR}]$, $[g_{iL}, g_{iR}]$, and $[b_{iL}, b_{iR}]$ are all interval valued system reliability, ith constraint, and ith resource, respectively. The sign $'\leq'$ is either $'<_{\min}'$ or $('=')$.

3.2 Constraint satisfaction rule

Here, we shall discuss the constraint satisfaction rule (i.e., under what conditions the interval form of constraints is satisfied). It should be noted that both sides of the constraints are in the interval form. For any solution $\bar{x}$ of (3), the ith constraint $[g_{iL}(x), g_{iR}(x)] \leq [b_{iL}, b_{iR}]$ ($i = 1, 2, \cdots, m$) will be satisfied if the condition either (a) or (b) given below is satisfied:

(a) $g_{iL}(\bar{x}) = b_{iL}$ and $g_{iR}(\bar{x}) = b_{iR}$ (when both the intervals $[g_{iL}(\bar{x}), g_{iR}(\bar{x})]$ and $[b_{iL}, b_{iR}]$ are equal).
(b) $[g_{iL}(\bar{x}), g_{iR}(\bar{x})] <_{\min} [b_{iL}, b_{iR}]$ when $[g_{iL}(\bar{x}), g_{iR}(\bar{x})]$ is less than $[b_{iL}, b_{iR}]$.

Again, the condition $[g_{iL}(\bar{x}), g_{iR}(\bar{x})] <_{\min} [b_{iL}, b_{iR}]$ will be satisfied if the following conditions hold good:

(i) $g_{iR}(\bar{x}) < b_{iL}$ (when $[g_{iL}(\bar{x}), g_{iR}(\bar{x})]$ and $[b_{iL}, b_{iR}]$ are Type-I intervals).
(ii) $g_{iL}(\bar{x}) < b_{iL}$, $g_{iR}(\bar{x}) \geq b_{iL}$, and $g_{iR}(\bar{x}) < b_{iR}$ (when $[g_{iL}(\bar{x}), g_{iR}(\bar{x})]$ and $[b_{iL}, b_{iR}]$ are Type-II intervals).
(iii) either $g_{iL}(\bar{x}) + g_{iR}(\bar{x}) \leq b_{iL} + b_{iR}$ and $g_{iR}(\bar{x}) - g_{iL}(\bar{x}) < b_{iR} - b_{iL}$, or $g_{iL}(\bar{x}) + g_{iR}(\bar{x}) \leq b_{iL} + b_{iR}$ and $g_{iL}(\bar{x}) < b_{iL}$ (when $[g_{iL}(\bar{x}), g_{iR}(\bar{x})]$ and $[b_{iL}, b_{iR}]$ are Type-III intervals).

4. Solution procedure: Genetic algorithm-based constrained handling approach

Undoubtedly, the problem (3) is very complex in nature. To solve this problem, we have utilized the Big-M penalty function technique [21, 23]. It is worth mentioning that the problem (3) is converted into its equivalent unconstrained optimization problem as follows:

$$\text{Maximize } [\overline{R}_{SL}(x), \overline{R}_{SR}(x)] = \begin{cases} [R_{SL}(x), R_{SR}(x)] & \text{when } x \in S \\ [-M, -M] & \text{when } x \notin S \end{cases} \tag{4}$$

where $S = \{x : [g_{iL}(x), g_{ir}(x)] \leq [b_{iL}, b_{iR}], i = 1, 2, \ldots, m; 1 \leq l_j \leq x_j \leq u_j; x_j \text{ is integer}, j = 1, \ldots, n\}$.

The problem (4) cannot be solved by use of any existing classical optimization technique due to its complicated structures. However, problem (4) might be solved by any heuristic/meta-heuristic algorithm. In this work, we have employed real coded GA together with an interval valued fitness function.

GAs [14] are all-purpose population-based search techniques that resemble the natural selection and natural genetics discussed by Charles Darwin. A GA can deftly be applied to solve a wide range of problems through the medium of a computer program. More elaborated discussion in reference to GAs is available in the book written by Gen and Cheng [34].

For implementation of the GA, the vital steps are as follows:

(i) setting of GA parameters P_s (population size), M_g (maximum number of generations), P_c (crossover probability), P_m (mutation rate), and confines of the decision variables;
(ii) encoding of solutions;
(iii) initialization of population;
(iv) fitness function evaluation;
(v) chromosomes selection;

(vi) offspring generation by crossover operation;
(vii) mutation operation on chromosomes; and.
(viii) termination condition.

The pseudo code of the proposed GA is given below:
Algorithm

> **INPUT:** *Decision variables with their bounds, P_s, M_g, P_c, and P_m;*
> **BEGIN.**
> *Set $T \leftarrow 0$ (T denotes generation/iteration number);*
> *Generate random population $P(T)$;*
> *Evaluate the fitness values of each chromosome of $P(T)$;*
> *Select the best chromosome from $P(T)$ according to the fitness value;*
> **WHILE** $(T \leq M_g)$ DO.
> > **BEGIN.**
> > *Set $T \leftarrow T + 1$;*
> > *Apply tournament selection process on $P(t-1)$ and select $P(T)$;*
> > *Apply crossover operation on $P(T)$ and create new $P(t)$;*
> > *Apply mutation operation on $P(t)$ and create new $P(t)$;*
> > *Evaluate the fitness values of each chromosome of $P(T)$;*
> > *Select the best chromosome from $P(T)$ according to the fitness value;*
> > *Compare the best chromosomes of $P(t)$ and $P(t-1)$ and set aside the better one;*
> > **END**
>
> **OUTPUT:** *Finest chromosome together with its corresponding fitness value;*
> **END**

Next we shall discuss three major operators of the GA: selection operator, crossover, and mutation.

The main purpose of the selection operator is to allow biasness to the better solutions and eradicate below-average solutions from the whole population for the succeeding generation. Here, the tournament selection process [23] of size two with replacement has been taken into account.

In the wake of the selection process, a crossover operation is performed to pick out the chromosomes that have remained. It is regarded as the main search operator of the GA. In the process of crossover, the genetic information between two or more individuals/chromosomes/solutions is combined to yield new solutions. In this GA, we have used a well-known intermediate crossover. Assume that $C_k^{(T)}$ and $C_i^{(T)}$ are two chromosomes that are selected randomly from $P(T)$. After recombination of the parent's solutions $C_k^{(T)}$ and $C_i^{(T)}$, the jth components/genes are as follows:

$$\overline{c}_{kj}^{(T)} = \begin{cases} c_{kj}^{(T)} - \rho & \text{if } c_{kj}^{(T)} > c_{ij}^{(T)} \\ c_{kj}^{(T)} + \rho & \text{otherwise} \end{cases} \quad \text{and} \quad \overline{c}_{ij}^{(t)} = \begin{cases} c_{ij}^{(T)} + \rho & \text{if } c_{kj}^{(T)} > c_{ij}^{(T)} \\ c_{ij}^{(T)} - \rho & \text{otherwise} \end{cases}$$

where ρ is a random integer generated from $U(0, |c_{kj}^{(T)} - c_{ij}^{(T)}|)$, $j = 1, 2, \ldots, n$.

The mutation operator enacts a vital role in the GA. This operator is executed after crossover and is applied to a single chromosome only. Here, we have used well-known one-neighborhood mutation

[23]. Suppose that $C_i^{(T)}$ is a single chromosome that is selected randomly from $P(T)$. After mutation, the kth component $c_{ik}^{(t)} \in [l_{ik}, u_{ik}]$ of $C_i^{(T)}$ is mutated as follows:

$$c_{ik}'^{(T)} = \begin{cases} c_{ik}^{(T)} + 1 & \text{if } c_{ik}^{(T)} = l_{ik} \\ c_{ik}^{(T)} - 1 & \text{if } c_{ik}^{(T)} = u_{ik} \\ c_{ik}^{(T)} + 1 & \text{if } \rho_1 < 0.5 \\ c_{ik}^{(T)} - 1 & \text{if } \rho_1 \geq 0.5 \end{cases}$$

where ρ_1 is a random number that lies between 0 and 1.

The fitness function is considered to regulate the fitness value of each solution candidate. In our proposed GA, the objective function of problem (4) has been considered as the fitness function.

At the time of execution of the GA, there is a possibility that the best solution may be missing from the population when a new population is fabricated by the process of crossover and mutation operations. To get the better of this issue, the wreck solution of the present generation is replaced by the best solutions of foregoing generation. Rather than a single solution/chromosome, more than one solution may be involved in this affair. This is known as elitism with size one.

In a GA, all the genetic operators are worked in a repeated way until a preset stopping criterion is reached. Here, we have considered the stopping criterion as the number of iteration/generations reaching the maximum number of generations.

---

5. Numerical example

In this section, a bridge network reliability system has been considered for illustration purposes (see Fig. 1). Here, we have assessed that all the design parameters relating to the problem (e.g., reliability of each component, available resources) are TFNs. This mentioned network system is made up of five subsystems and three nonlinear and nonseparable constraints. The subsystems have parallel options, or two out of n: G structure with fuzzy valued reliabilities of components. The overall system reliability $\tilde{R}_S$ is as follows:

$$\tilde{R}_S = \tilde{R}_5 \left(1 - \tilde{Q}_1 \tilde{Q}_3\right)\left(1 - \tilde{Q}_2 \tilde{Q}_4\right) + \tilde{Q}_5 \left[1 - \left(1 - \tilde{R}_1 \tilde{R}_2\right)\left(1 - \tilde{R}_3 \tilde{R}_4\right)\right]$$

where $\tilde{R}_j = \tilde{R}_j(x_j)$ and $\tilde{Q}_j(x_j) = 1 - \tilde{R}_j$ for all $j = 1, 2, 3, 4, 5$. Since the system has a complex structure, the objective function is also nonlinear and nonseparable. The mathematical formulation of the problem is given below:

[P1]: Maximize $\tilde{R}_S = \tilde{R}_5 \left(1 - \tilde{Q}_1 \tilde{Q}_3\right)\left(1 - \tilde{Q}_2 \tilde{Q}_4\right) + \tilde{Q}_5 \left[1 - \left(1 - \tilde{R}_1 \tilde{R}_2\right)\left(1 - \tilde{R}_3 \tilde{R}_4\right)\right]$.

subject to:

$$(8, 10, 11)\exp\left(\frac{x_1}{2}\right)x_2 + (19, 20, 21)x_3 + (2.5, 3, 3.2)x_4^2 + (7.5, 8, 9)x_5 \leq (195, 200, 202);$$

$$(8, 10, 11)\exp\left(\frac{x_1}{2}\right) + (3.5, 4, 4.2)\exp(x_2) + (1.5, 2, 3)x_3^3 + (5, 6, 7)\left[x_4^2 + \exp\left(\frac{x_4}{4}\right)\right]$$

$$+ (6.5, 7, 7.3)\exp\left(\frac{x_5}{4}\right) \leq (300, 310, 315); (11.5, 12, 13)\left[x_2^2 + \exp(x_2)\right] + (4, 5, 5.5)x_3 \exp\left(\frac{x_3}{4}\right)$$

$$+ (2.5, 3, 3.2)x_1 x_4^2 + (1.5, 2, 3)x_5^3 \leq (518, 520, 525); (1, 1, 1, 1, 1) \leq (x_1, x_2, x_3, x_4, x_5) \leq (6, 3, 5, 6, 6);$$

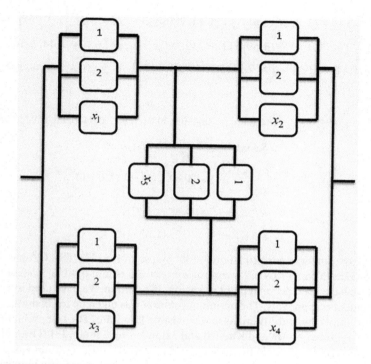

FIG. 1

A complex bridge network system.

where

$$\tilde{R}_1(x_1) = \{(.7, .8, .83), (.84, .85, .86), (.86, .90, .92), (.900, .925, .950), (.93, .95, .97), (.972, .975, .978)\};$$

$$\tilde{R}_2(x_2) = 1 - (1 - (0.72, 0.75, 0.76))^{x_2};$$

$$\tilde{R}_3(x_3) = \sum_{k=2}^{x_3+1} \binom{x_3+1}{k} ((0.86, 0.88, 0.89))^k ([0.11, 0.12, 0.14))^{x_3+1-k};$$

$$\tilde{R}_4(x_4) = 1 - (1 - (0.69, 0.70, 0.72))^{x_4};$$

$$\tilde{R}_5(x_5) = 1 - (1 - (0.84, 0.85, 0.86))^{x_5};$$

It should be noted that the problem [P1] along with numerical data has been taken from the paper studied by Sahoo [35].

Now, using the DCN and its corresponding interval number, the above problem can be written as follows:

[P2]: Maximize $R_S = [R_{SL}, R_{SU}]$.

subject to

$$[8.88, 11.12] \exp\left(\frac{x_1}{2}\right) x_2 + [19.29, 20.71]x_3 + [2.73, 3.27]x_4{}^2 + [7.44, 8.56]x_5 \leq [197.31, 202.69]$$

$$[8.88, 11.12] \exp\left(\frac{x_1}{2}\right) + [3.73, 4.27] \exp(x_2) + [1.44, 2.56]x_3{}^3 + [5.29, 6.71]\left[x_4{}^2 + \exp\left(\frac{x_4}{4}\right)\right]$$
$$+ [6.71, 7.29] \exp\left(\frac{x_5}{4}\right) \leq [304.41, 315.59], [11.44, 12.56]\left[x_2{}^2 + \exp(x_2)\right] + [4.44, 5.56]x_3 \exp\left(\frac{x_3}{4}\right)$$
$$+ [2.73, 3.27]x_1 x_4{}^2 + [1.44, 2.56]x_5{}^3 \leq [517.31, 522.69], (1, 1, 1, 1, 1) \leq (x_1, x_2, x_3, x_4, x_5) \leq (6, 3, 5, 6, 6),$$

where

$$\tilde{R}_1(x_1) = \{[0.75, 0.85], [0.84, 0.86], [0.88, 0.92], [0.91, 0.94], [0.94, 0.96], [0.97, 0.98]\};$$

$$\tilde{R}_2(x_2) = 1 - (1 - [0.73, 0.77])^{x_2};$$

$$\tilde{R}_3(x_3) = \sum_{k=2}^{x_3+1} \binom{x_3+1}{k}([0.87, 0.89])^k (1 - [0.87, 0.89])^{x_3+1-k};$$

$$\tilde{R}_4(x_4) = 1 - (1 - [0.69, 0.71])^{x_4};$$

$$\tilde{R}_5(x_5) = 1 - (1 - [0.84, 0.86])^{x_5};$$

Next, a numerical experiment is performed on the P2 by use of the GA. This GA has been coded in C and run with a 2.5 GHz PC on a LINUX operating system. To obtain optimal system reliability, in all the computations we have used decimal point precision. In addition, we have used integer precision for obtaining the redundant components. The optimum solution was taken up to six digits after the decimal point to manage the similarity with solutions in the existing literature. The test problem assumed in this work was initially suggested by Ha and Kuo [6] and extended by Sahoo [35]. Throughout the computation, 50 trials were carried out to obtain the best solution, which is the optimal value of the objective function and optimal numbers of redundant components. For the purpose of a numerical experiment, the values of parameters, viz. population size, maximum no. of generations, probability of crossover, and probability of mutation, have been taken as 100, 100, 0.85, and 0.15, respectively. The terminating rule was fixed (i.e., when the iterations of the computation reached 100). The similarities of the results between the proposed approach and other approaches, viz. fuzzy approach [35, 36], branch and bound approach [6], and a heuristic [37], are displayed in Table 1. In all the studies except the proposed approach, it may be noticed that all results are precise numbers. However, our proposed study provides a deterministic interval, which is the expected range of the optimal system reliability. Moreover, when we have solved the original one studied by Ha and Kuo [6] using our proposed approach, we have obtained a precise reliability value, which has been presented in the second row of Table 1. From this

Table 1 Computational results.

Environment	x^*	R_S^*	CPU time (in s)	Method/algorithm used
Fuzzy and DCN	(3,1,2,3,3)	**[0.991739, 0.999478]**	0.04	Our proposed approach
Crisp	(3,2,4,4,2)	**0.999382**	0.04	Our proposed approach
Fuzzy	(1,3,4,3,3)	0.999330	0.08	Sahoo [35]
Fuzzy	(1,3,4,3,3)	0.999306	0.06	Sahoo & Mahato [36]
Crisp	(1,3,4,3,3)	0.999373	–	Branch and bound [6]
Crisp	(2,2,4,4,2)	0.999327	–	GAG heuristic [28, 37]

table, it may be observed that the best optimal solution has been obtained by our approach proposed in this study.

Therefore, we have concluded that the proposed method finds a global optimum solution in terms of interval (i.e., it gives the expected range of the system reliability, and the computational results demonstrate that the prescribed approach is able to grasp several complex problems and constraints in terms of interval parametric values). It can be seen that the suggested approach is very well organized, compared with other approaches, in terms of system reliability. Thus, we confirmed that the prescribed approach is foremost out of the familiar existing approaches to handle the RRAP under fuzziness.

6. Concluding remarks

In this chapter, a new concept for figure out the RRAPs under fuzziness has been presented. Due to some unexpected conditions, the reliability of each component and other design parameters relating to the system are depicted in the shape of a TFN by taking into account the uncertainty/fuzziness. Using the concept of dual-connection numbers, the TFN has been converted into an interval number; using this interval number, in this chapter we have constructed the RRAP in the form of an interval-valued optimization problem. This representation is more appropriate because one may easily solve the same by using interval order relations and the GA. In the end, a computative example was resolved and a computational result was presented. The computational result indicated that the optimal system reliability acquired from our suggested approach is more flexible than the others. The proposed approach also has some disadvantages. These are: (i) no one can solve the problem manually (hand calculations); (ii) space complexity is very large; and (iii) several procedures are required to implement the approach. For further studies, one may implement the whole approach to unravel decision-making problems in the fields of uncertain optimization, manufacturing design, business science, etc.

References

[1] F.A. Tillman, C.L. Hwang, W. Kuo, Optimization technique for system reliability with redundancy: a review, IEEE Trans. Reliab. 26 (1977) 148–155.

[2] W. Kuo, V.R. Prasad, An annotated overview of system-reliability optimization, IEEE Trans. Reliab. 49 (2001) 176–187.

[3] Y. Nakagawa, K.A. Nakashima, Heuristic method for determining optimal reliability allocation, IEEE Trans. Reliab. 26 (3) (1977) 156–161.

[4] J.H. Kim, B.J.A. Yum, Heuristic method for solving redundancy optimization problems in complex systems, IEEE Trans. Reliab. 42 (4) (1993) 572–578.

[5] K.K. Aggarwal, J.S. Gupta, Penalty function approach in heuristic algorithms for constrained, IEEE Trans. Reliab. 54 (3) (2005) 549–558.

[6] C. Ha, W. Kuo, Reliability redundancy allocation: an improved realization for nonconvex nonlinear programming problems, Eur. J. Oper. Res. 171 (2006) 124–138.

[7] W. Kuo, H. Lin, Z. Xu, W. Zhang, Reliability optimization with the Lagrange- multiplier and branch-and-bound technique, IEEE Trans. Reliab. 36 (1987) 624–630.

[8] X.L. Sun, D. Li, Optimization condition and branch and bound algorithm for constrained redundancy optimization in series system, Optim. Eng. 3 (2002) 53–65.

[9] C.S. Sung, Y.K. Cho, Branch and bound redundancy optimization for a series system with multiple-choice constraints, IEEE Trans. Reliab. 48 (1999) 108–117.

[10] C.L. Hwang, F.A. Tillman, W. Kuo, Reliability optimization by generalized lagrangian-function based and reduced-gradient methods, IEEE Trans. Reliab. 28 (1979) 316–319.

[11] K.B. Misra, U. Sharma, An efficient algorithm to solve integer- programming problems arising in system-reliability design, IEEE Trans. Reliab. 40 (1991) 81–91.

[12] Y. Nakagawa, S. Miyazaki, Surrogate constraints algorithm for reliability optimization problems with two constraints, IEEE Trans. Reliab. 30 (1981) 175–180.

[13] M. Hikita, K. Nakagawa, K. Nakashima, H. Narihisa, Reliability optimization of systems by a surrogate-constraints algorithm, IEEE Trans. Reliab. 41 (3) (1992) 473–480.

[14] D.E. Goldberg, Genetic Algorithms: Search, Optimization and Machine Learning, Addison Wesley, Reading, MA, 1989.

[15] H. Garg, An efficient biogeography based optimization algorithm for solving reliability optimization problems, Swarm Evol. Comput. 24 (2015) 1–10.

[16] H. Garg, An approach for solving constrained reliability-redundancy allocation problems using cuckoo search algorithm, Beni-Suef Univ. J. Basic Appl. Sci. 4 (1) (2015) 14–25.

[17] H. Garg, M. Rani, S.P. Sharma, Y. Vishwakarma, Bi-objective optimization of the reliability-redundancy allocation problem for series-parallel system, J. Manuf. Syst. 33 (3) (2014) 335–347.

[18] H. Garg, S.P. Sharma, Multi-objective reliability-redundancy allocation problem using particle swarm optimization, Comput. Ind. Eng. 64 (1) (2013) 247–255.

[19] H. Garg, M. Rani, S.P. Sharma, An efficient two phase approach for solving reliability–redundancy allocation problem using artificial bee colony technique, Comput. Oper. Res. 40 (12) (2013) 2961–2969.

[20] L.A. Zadeh, Fuzzy sets, Infect. Control 8 (3) (1965) 338–352.

[21] R.K. Gupta, A.K. Bhunia, D. Roy, A GA based penalty function technique for solving constrained redundancy allocation problem of series system with interval valued reliabilities of components, J. Comput. Appl. Math. 232 (2009) 275–284.

[22] L. Sahoo, A.K. Bhunia, P.K. Kapur, Genetic algorithm based multi-objective reliability optimization in interval environment, Comput. Ind. Eng. 62 (2012) 152–160.

[23] A.K. Bhunia, L. Sahoo, D. Roy, Reliability stochastic optimization for a series system with interval component reliability via genetic algorithm, Appl. Math Comput. 216 (2010) 929–939.

[24] H. Garg, M. Rani, S.P. Sharma, Y. Vishwakarma, Intuitionistic fuzzy optimization technique for solving multi-objective reliability optimization problems in interval environment, Expert Syst. Appl. 41 (7) (2014) 3157–3167.

[25] I. Irvanizam, T. Usman, M. Iqbal, T. Iskandar, M. Marzuki, An extended fuzzy TODIM approach for multiple-attribute decision-making with dual-connection numbers, Adv. Fuzzy Syst. 2020 (2020) 1–10.

[26] H. Garg, K. Kumar, Power geometric aggregation operators based on connection number of set pair analysis under intuitionistic fuzzy environment, Arab. J. Sci. Eng. 45 (3) (2019) 2049–2063.

[27] H. Garg, K. Kumar, A novel exponential distance and its based TOPSIS method for interval-valued intuitionistic fuzzy sets using connection number of SPA theory, Artif. Intell. Rev. 1 (1) (2018) 1–20.

[28] S. Fu, H. Zhou, Triangular fuzzy number multi-attribute decision-making method based on set-pair analysis, J. Softw. Eng. 11 (1) (2017) 116–122.

[29] R.E. Moore, Methods and Applications of Interval Analysis, SIAM, Philadelphia, 1979.

[30] R.E. Moore, R.B. Kearfott, M.J. Cloud, Introduction to Interval Analysis, SIAM, Philadelphia, 2009.

[31] E.R. Hansen, G.W. Walster, Global Optimization Using Interval Analysis, Marcel Dekker Inc, New York, 2004.

[32] S. Karmakar, S. Mahato, A.K. Bhunia, Interval oriented multi-section techniques for global optimization, J. Comput. Appl. Math. 224 (2009) 476–491.

[33] S.K. Mahato, A.K. Bhunia, Interval-arithmetic-oriented interval computing technique for global optimization, Appl. Math. Res. Exp. 2006 (2006) 1–19.

[34] M. Gen, R. Cheng, Genetic Algorithms and Engineering Optimization, John Wiley & Sons, 2000.

[35] L. Sahoo, Genetic algorithm based approach for reliability redundancy allocation problems in fuzzy environment, Int. J. Math. Eng. Manage. Sci. 2 (4) (2017) 259–272.

[36] L. Sahoo, S. Mahato, Optimal redundancy allocation for bridge network system with fuzzy parameters, J. Appl. Quant. Methods 13 (1) (2018).

[37] K. Gopal, K.K. Aggarwal, J.S. Gupta, An improved algorithm for reliability optimization, IEEE Trans. Reliab. 29 (1978) 325–328.

Index

Note: Page numbers followed by *f* indicate figures and *t* indicate tables.